LIVING ABUNDANTLY

A Study in Christian Stewardship

FRANK E. BURKHALTER
Former Professor of Journalism, Baylor University

Convention Press
NASHVILLE   TENNESSEE

Printed in the United States of America
5. 8 59 R.R.D.

ABOUT THE AUTHOR

Frank E. Burkhalter is a native Texan. After graduating at Baylor University and Columbia University, he did daily newspaper work in Texas for several years, and then gave two years to the service of Texas A. & M. College as director of its publicity and editorial work.

From his post at A. & M. College he was called to Nashville to direct the publicity for the Baptist 75 Million Campaign in the fall of 1919, and continued in this work until September, 1929, when he was recalled to Baylor University to become head of that institution's department of journalism, a position he held until his retirement in 1947.

During the author's service with the Southern Baptist Convention he represented that body on the United Stewardship Council, composed of representatives of various evangelical denominations. He also wrote numerous tracts and booklets upon stewardship and various other phases of Christian service.

From early life Mr. Burkhalter has given large service to boys through the agencies of boys' clubs and the Intermediate classes of various Baptist Sunday schools. Out of this and other experiences grew his books *Publicity Handbook for Southern Baptists, Living Abundantly, Winning the Adolescent Boy,* a chapter in *The Centennial Story of Texas Baptists,* and *Intermediate Fishers.* For the past twenty-five years Mr. Burkhalter has written and spoken widely on the issue of international peace. He is a frequent contributor to the periodicals of the Baptist Sunday School Board.

ACKNOWLEDGMENTS

The following authors and publishers have graciously given permission for the use of copyrighted material. We acknowledge our appreciation

To the International Council of Religious Education for permission to use the American Standard Version of the Bible.

To Bishop Ralph S. Cushman for permission to quote the poem, "The Secret," from his book, *I Have a Stewardship*, The Abingdon Press.

To the Judson Press for permission to quote from *The Larger Stewardship*, by Charles A. Cook.

NOTE.—Unless otherwise indicated, all Scripture references are from the American Standard Version.

CHURCH STUDY COURSE
FOR TEACHING AND TRAINING

The Church Study Course for Teaching and Training began October 1, 1959. It is a merger of three courses previously promoted by the Baptist Sunday School Board—the Sunday School Training Course, the Graded Training Union Study Course, and the Church Music Training Course.

The course is fully graded. The system of awards provides a series of five diplomas of twenty books each for Adults or Young People, one diploma of ten books for Young People, two diplomas of five books each for Intermediates, and two diplomas of five books each for Juniors. All book awards earned previously in the Sunday School Training Course, the Graded Training Union Study Course, and the Church Music Training Course may be transferred to the new course.

The course is comprehensive. The books are arranged in nineteen categories. The purpose of the course is to help Christians to grow in knowledge and conviction, to help them to grow toward maturity in Christian character and competence for service, to encourage them to participate worthily as workers in their churches, and to develop leaders for all phases of church life and work.

The Church Study Course for Teaching and Training is promoted by the Baptist Sunday School Board, 127 Ninth Avenue, North, Nashville, Tennessee, through its Sunday School, Training Union, Church Music, and Church Administration Departments and by the Sunday school, Training Union, and Church Music departments of the states affiliated with the Southern Baptist Convention. A complete description of the course and the system of awards may be found in the *Church Study Course for Teaching and Training* catalog which may be obtained without charge from any one of these departments.

A record of all awards earned should be maintained in each church. A person should be designated by the church to keep the files. Forms for such records may be ordered from any Baptist Book Store.

Requirements for credit for the study of this book may be found on page vii. This book provides credit in category 1, section A.

▼

REQUIREMENTS FOR CREDIT
IN CLASS OR HOME STUDY

If credit is desired for the study of this book in a class or by home study the following requirements must be met:

I. IN CLASSWORK

1. The class must meet a minimum of seven and one-half hours. The required time does not include assembly periods. Ten class periods of forty-five minutes each are recommended. (If laboratory or clinical work is desired in specialized or technical courses, this requirement may be met by six clock hours of classwork and three clock hours of supervised laboratory or clinical work.)

2. A class member who attends all class sessions and completes the reading of the book within a week following the last class session will not be required to do any written work.

3. A class member who is absent from one or more sessions must answer the questions on all chapters he misses. In such a case, he must turn in his paper within a week and must certify that the book has been read.

4. The teacher should request an award for himself. A person who teaches a book in Sections B, C, or D of any category or conducts an approved unit of instruction for Nursery, Beginner, or Primary children will be granted an award in Category 11, Special Studies, which will count as an elective on his own diploma. He should specify in his request the name of the book taught, or the unit conducted for Nursery, Beginners, or Primaries.

5. The teacher should complete the Request for Book Award—Class Study (Form 150) and forward it within two weeks after the completion of the class to the Church Study Course Awards Office, 127 Ninth Avenue, North, Nashville 3, Tennessee.

II. IN HOME STUDY

1. A person who does not attend any class session may receive credit by answering all questions for written work as indicated in the book. When a person turns in his paper on home study, he must certify that he has read the book.

2. Students may find profit in studying the text together, but individual papers are required. Carbon copies or duplicates in any form cannot be accepted.

3. Home study work papers may be graded by the pastor or a person designated by him or they may be sent to the Church Study Course Awards Office for grading. The form Request for Book Award—Home Study (Form 151) must be used in requesting awards. It should be mailed to Church Study Course Awards Office, 127 Ninth Avenue, North, Nashville 3, Tennessee.

III. CREDIT FOR THIS BOOK

This book is No. 0109 in category 1, section A.

CONTENTS

CHAPTER I

THE ABUNDANT LIFE

If you should ask all Christians you know if they wished to be happy, the universal response would be an emphatic "I do." But if you should inquire of them if they are genuinely happy today, the number of sincere, positive replies would doubtless be small indeed.

Why are there so few radiantly happy Christians in proportion to the total number of professed disciples in the world? While numerous reasons might be offered, all the more fundamental ones would center around the fact that the average Christian is unwilling to pay the price of the highest joy. This average Christian is still under the delusion that he can serve two masters; he prefers the husks of an indifferent life to the solid, satisfying food enjoyed by him who lives the abundant life; and he has not yet attained that growth in spiritual stature where he is willing to substitute God's will in his life for his own.

James, the brother of our Lord, evidently had this type of Christian in mind when he observed, "Ye have not, because ye ask not. Ye ask, and receive not, because ye ask amiss, that ye may spend it in your pleasures" (James 4: 2-3). Likewise our Lord sought to win the unfruitful Christian to the abundant life when he exhorted: "If any man would come after me, let him deny himself, and take up his cross, and follow me. For whosoever would save his life shall lose it: and whosoever shall lose his life for my sake shall find it. For what shall a man be profited, if he shall gain the whole world, and forfeit his life? or what shall a man give in exchange for his life?" (Matt. 16: 24-26).

Christ not only expounded the principles of the abundant life in his teachings; he was able also to testify out of his rich experience that "it is more blessed to give than to receive" (Acts 20:35) and, "Give, and it shall be given unto you; good measure, pressed down, shaken together, running over, shall they give into your bosom. For with what measure ye mete it shall be measured to you again" (Luke 6:38).

To this testimony of our Saviour should be added that of his greatest follower of all the ages, Paul, who wrote, "He that soweth sparingly shall reap also sparingly; and he that soweth bountifully shall reap also bountifully" (2 Cor. 9:6).

It is only the Christian who is willing to invest all his resources in the service of God who can expect to live the abounding, radiantly happy life.

I. CHRISTIANS ARE GOD'S STEWARDS

Before any Christian can live the abundant life, however, he must recognize that he is a steward of God, and that his happiness will be in proportion to the faithfulness with which he assumes and discharges that stewardship. A steward is one of God's trusted servants to whom he has delegated responsibility in helping promote his kingdom in the earth.

II. WHAT DOES STEWARDSHIP INVOLVE?

What does our relation to God as stewards involve? is a proper question. This relationship, with all its logical implications, is too extensive a subject to cover fully, even in a whole book; and we shall be able to suggest here only a few of the more fundamental of those principles. They are:

1. We are not our own, but God's.

2. Our first duty as stewards is to know and do God's will.

3. All the talents, resources, and opportunities that we possess have been entrusted to us by the Heavenly Father to be employed in his service along whatever channels he may direct.

4. God's claims upon us take precedence over every other obligation of any type.

5. Our responsibility and duty are determined by our ability and by our Father's will for us, regardless of what his purpose for our neighbors or friends may be.

6. God makes no impossible, unreasonable demands upon his stewards.

III. WE ARE NOT OUR OWN, BUT GOD'S

Underlying every study of our relationship and duty to God is that fundamental truth so emphatically set forth by Paul, "Ye are not your own; for ye were bought with a price" (1 Cor. 6:19-20).

Why do we belong to God? Various reasons could be cited, but this study is concerned with basic ideas only. There are three fundamental reasons why this relationship exists: We are God's by his right of creation, by his right of redemption, and by reason of his providential care for us.

1. *We Are God's by Creation*

It is a bit difficult for us freeborn Americans of this generation, enjoying, perhaps, the largest political, economic, social, and religious liberty ever conferred upon any people of the world—a liberty that has cost us nothing—to realize that in truth we are not our own, but God's.

In the biblical record of creation, after the Father had called into being the heavenly bodies, the firmament, the waters, the dry land, and animal and vegetable life of every variety, he addressed the other members of the Godhead thus: "Let us make man in our image, after our likeness: and let them have dominion over the fish of the sea, and over the birds of the heavens, and over the cattle, and over all the earth, and over every creeping thing that creepeth upon the earth" (Gen. 1:26). And after God had created man he gave him this firsthand commission: "And God blessed them: and God said unto them, Be fruitful, and multiply, and replenish the earth, and subdue it" (Gen. 1: 28).

There are few subjects that we Christians of today need to restudy more carefully than the fact and purpose of our creation at the hands of the Almighty and the way we are measuring up to his expectations of us. Evidently David had a much better conception of our exalted relationship to our Creator than most of us enjoy, when he sang,

> When I consider thy heavens, the work of thy fingers,
> The moon and the stars, which thou hast ordained;
> What is man, that thou art mindful of him?
> And the son of man, that thou visitest him?
> For thou hast made him but little lower than God,
> And crownest him with glory and honor (Psalm 8: 3-5).

Of all the great men in the Bible, probably none knew God and his relationship to mankind quite so fully as did Paul, and surely none dedicated himself more wholeheartedly to fulfilling God's purpose for his life than did the great Apostle to the Gentiles. Out of this knowledge of God and his will, Paul was able to pen this vital plank in the platform of every true Christian steward: "For whether we live, we live unto the Lord; or whether we die, we die unto the Lord: whether we live therefore, or die, we are the Lord's" (Rom. 14:8).

2. *We Are God's by Right of Redemption*

Unfortunately, man did not fully appreciate the high estate which God conferred upon him by creating him in his own image and then entrusting to his hands the occupation and the subjugation of the whole earth for the Creator's glory. For it was not long after his creation that man allowed Satan to seduce him into sin and denial of his Maker. This disobedience terminated the intimate fellowship which man up until this time had enjoyed with Jehovah.

But in spite of the fall, God loved man and revealed that love by sending his only begotten Son into the world, to offer himself on the cross as a perfect sacrifice for the sins of the race.

All of us can repeat from memory the key verse of the gospel, but we need to meditate upon it frequently: "For God so loved the world, that he gave his only begotten Son, that whosoever believeth on him should not perish, but have eternal life" (John 3:16).

All who have been carefully instructed recognize that one can be saved only through the exercise of his personal faith in Jesus Christ. This doctrine was made explicit by Paul: "For by grace have ye been saved through faith; and that not of yourselves, it is the gift of God; not of works, that no man should glory" (Eph. 2:8-9). That there is absolutely nothing we can do to buy salvation is explained further by Paul: "The free gift of God is eternal life in Christ Jesus our Lord" (Rom. 6:23).

As you have been redeemed therefore through faith in God's only begotten Son, how true is the declaration of the inspired apostle that "Ye are not your own; for ye were bought with a price" (1 Cor. 6:19-20)!

3. We Are God's by His Providential Provision for Us

There is a decided disposition on the part of the average individual to regard everything he possesses as definitely his own, to do with it absolutely as he pleases. However, this position cannot be maintained in the light of God's Word. No single truth is more positively sustained by Bible teaching than that every resource we have is the gift of God. In fact, the teachings of the Book upon this point are so clear and positive that they require no special comment to enable the sincere Christian to recognize their import. A few brief passages are cited:

For in him we live, and move, and have our being (Acts 17:28).

Seeing he himself giveth to all life, and breath and all things (Acts 17:25).

What hast thou that thou didst not receive? (1 Cor. 4:7).

For we brought nothing into the world, for neither can we carry anything out (1 Tim. 6:7).

The earth is Jehovah's, and the fulness thereof;
The world, and they that dwell therein (Psalm 24:1).

For every beast of the forest is mine,
And the cattle upon a thousand hills (Psalm 50:10).

The silver is mine, and the gold is mine, saith Jehovah of hosts (Hag. 2:8).

And yet he left not himself without witness, in that he did good and gave you from heaven rains and fruitful seasons, filling your hearts with food and gladness (Acts 14:17).

Someone who has made a careful study of Christian stewardship has calculated that at least 95 per cent of the factors entering into the production of wealth are contributed by God and society, and only 5 per cent by ourselves. Among the contributions listed in this tabulation as having been made by God are our bodies, minds, and health, the soil, the climate, and all the mineral, agricultural, and livestock resources of the earth; and society contributes the markets and the bulk of the transportation facilities, though the seas and the rivers are also furnished by the Creator. The 5 per cent which we ourselves contribute toward the production of wealth is represented by the will to work.

Recognition of the fact that all we have and are is the gift of God, in one form or another, is absolutely essential to a correct understanding of stewardship. Moreover, such recognition must come before one can begin to grow in Christian character and find joy and usefulness in the Christian life.

IV. WE MUST TAKE ORDERS FROM GOD

Since we are not our own, but God's, it is logical, proper, and necessary that we take orders from him. The attitude of David, the happiest of all characters in the Old Testament, in finding perennial joy in obeying God's will, should characterize all Christians of this day. In this connection, it is interesting to note that the Lord expressed his appreciation of David's loyalty by designating him as a man after God's own heart.

There are numerous Bible passages emphasizing the fact that we, as Christians, must take orders from God rather than man and must give his orders priority over all other claims; but only a few of the more emphatic ones are cited here to establish the point:

What doth Jehovah thy God require of thee, but to fear Jehovah thy God, to walk in all his ways, and to love him, and to serve Jehovah thy God with all thy heart and with all thy soul, to keep the commandments of Jehovah, and his statutes, which I command thee this day for thy good? (Deut. 10:12-13).

Behold, I set before you this day a blessing and a curse: the blessing, if ye shall hearken unto the commandments of Jehovah your God, which I command you this day; and the curse, if ye shall not hearken unto the commandments of Jehovah your God (Deut. 11:26-28).

Then saith Jesus unto him, Get thee hence, Satan: for it is written, Thou shalt worship the Lord thy God, and him only shalt thou serve (Matt. 4:10).

And he saith unto them, Come ye after me, and I will make you fishers of men (Matt. 4:19).

All authority hath been given unto me in heaven and on earth. Go ye therefore, and make disciples of all the nations, baptizing them into the name of the Father and of the Son and of the Holy Spirit: teaching them to observe all things whatsoever I commanded you: and lo, I am with you always, even unto the end of the world (Matt. 28:18-20).

If any man would come after me, let him deny himself, and take up his cross, and follow me. For whosoever would save his life shall lose it; and whosoever shall lose his life for my sake and the gospel's shall save it (Mark 8:34-35).

As the Father hath sent me, even so send I you (John 20:21).

We must obey God rather than men (Acts 5:29).

In a study of the penalties of disobedience and the blessings of obedience, may we not draw an analogy from our own childhood in our relations to our parents? This writer recalls vividly how, when he flagrantly disobeyed the orders of his parents, his conscience smote him before this disobedience ever came to the attention of his father or mother; and he regretted his disloyalty before he had received the parental reprimand and punishment. On the other hand, he is reminded of the satisfaction he found in the ease of conscience that was his, even before he had heard his parents' approval, resultant from duty well performed.

But how much more satisfying is the approval of the Heavenly Father than the commendation of an earthly parent, and how much richer are the rewards which the Lord confers upon loyal Christians than any benefit which earthly fathers and mothers could possibly bestow upon their children!

And just as a child is frequently disposed to think his parents' commands are unduly stern, so children of God frequently complain about the rigid exactions of the Christian life. But just as true parents discipline their children because they love them and wish to help them develop the best type of character, so God calls upon his stewards to forsake the world and live the separated life because he knows that only thus will they grow stronger spiritually, most faithfully typify the Saviour whose name they bear, and prove most useful in extending God's kingdom in the world.

Just as Christ promised his presence and power to those who went forth in obedience to his commission to evangelize the world, so throughout the Bible we find the Father's choicest blessings are conditioned upon our doing his will.

V. ALL OUR ABILITIES ARE GIVEN BY GOD

Not only did God create us, place us in this beautiful and well-endowed world, provide for our redemption when we lost our first high estate through sin, and provide us with all the material blessings which the world affords us, but also he gave to us all the talents and abilities which we possess. And since an all-wise and all-good Heavenly Father never does anything thoughtlessly, his conferring upon us peculiar fitness for special tasks indicates that he is looking to us to perform those services for which he definitely equipped us. He is grieved when we fail to meet his expectations of us.

Let us examine a few Bible passages bearing upon the point under consideration:

Every good gift and every perfect gift is from above (James 1:17).

But thou shalt remember Jehovah thy God, for it is he that giveth thee power to get wealth (Deut. 8:18).

For it is as when a man, going into another country, called his own servants, and delivered unto them his goods. And unto one he gave five talents, to another two, to another one; to each according to his several ability; and he went on his journey (Matt. 25:14-15).

And God hath set some in the church, first apostles, secondly prophets, thirdly teachers, then miracles, then gifts of healings, helps, governments, divers kinds of tongues. Are all apostles? are all prophets? are all teachers? are all workers of miracles? have all gifts of healing? do all speak with tongues? do all interpret? (1 Cor. 12:28-30).

Of all the over two billion persons in the world, the scientists inform us that no two have exactly the same physical, mental, and psychological characteristics. We begin to realize the wisdom of God in ordaining this wide diversity, when we contemplate how our neighbors would get on our nerves if they were exact duplicates of ourselves and how monotonous society would be if we were all alike in appearance, gifts, and tastes.

More important than this consideration, however, is the fact that God has endowed each of us with his own special talents and abilities, and that he is looking to each of us individually to employ these abilities as efficiently as possible and in accordance with his will for our lives.

God expects some to preach, others to teach, and still others to minister to the needs of the race as physicians and nurses. He ordains that some engage in farming to produce the food for the sustenance of the race and that others engage in business. He expects all to support the preachers, missionaries, and others involved in the extension of his kingdom to the ends of the earth.

Southern Baptists are far more numerous than are the members of any other religious group in this section of the nation. In native gifts and abilities they are easily the equal of any other denomination. By reason of their larger numbers they have by far a greater combined wealth than any other sect. If all the members of all our churches were faithful stewards in the exercise of their gifts and the consecration of their means, Southern Baptists alone could send the knowledge of Jesus Christ to the whole world within one generation.

VI. God's Claims Come First

Since God is our Maker, our Redeemer, and the giver of every good and perfect gift, including individual talents and abilities, giving him anything less than first place in our affections and loyalties would violate the law of propriety, and would be unworthy of the character of God.

The priority of God's claims upon his children over our obligations to family, friends, or state, is emphasized throughout the Bible; but a few selected passages will suffice to establish the point:

He that loveth father or mother more than me is not worthy of me; and he that loveth son or daughter more than me is not worthy of me. And he that doth not take his cross and follow after me, is not worthy of me. He that findeth his life shall lose it; and he that loseth his life for my sake shall find it (Matt. 10: 37-39).

And Jesus said unto Simon, Fear not; from henceforth thou shalt catch men. And when they had brought their boats to land, they left all, and followed him (Luke 5:10-11).

I beseech you therefore, brethren, by the mercies of God, to present your bodies a living sacrifice, holy, acceptable to God, which is your spiritual service (Rom. 12:1).

But put ye on the Lord Jesus Christ, and make not provision for the flesh, to fulfil the lusts thereof (Rom. 13:14).

For whether we live, we live unto the Lord; or whether we die, we die unto the Lord: whether we live therefore, or die, we are the Lord's (Rom. 14:8).

So then each one of us shall give account of himself to God (Rom. 14:12).

The truly great and useful stewards and servants of God through the ages have been those of great faith and deep love who have counted it a privilege to bear burdens, endure hardships, and follow the will of the Lord at all costs. And while the world has regarded such hardships and sacrifices as foolish, the compensations which God has bestowed upon his faithful servants have made duty sweet indeed. Proof of this statement is presented in the eleventh chapter of Hebrews, the challenging roll call of God's heroes of faith.

When General William Booth, founder of the Salvation Army, was an old man, a journalist in the course of an interview asked him what he regarded as the secret of his greatness. "I cannot regard myself as great," this servant of needy people modestly replied, "but whatever measure of success I may have attained has been due to the fact that God has had all there is of me." Such dedication to God makes even the humblest Christian not only happy but great and useful; for when one places himself at the Lord's disposal, God comes into his life and fills it with his own grace and power.

VII. RESPONSIBILITY TO GOD IS PERSONAL

It has been previously pointed out in this discussion that there are no two persons in the world with exactly identical appearances, talents, and tastes. A natural corollary of this principle is that each one of God's creatures bears an individual responsibility to God for the manner in which he employs his natural endowments. How our friends exercise their talents is of small concern to us: our responsibility is to God.

In support of this general position let us turn to a few key passages from the Word of God:

Now the word of Jehovah came unto me, saying, Before I formed thee in the belly I knew thee, and before thou camest forth out of the womb I sanctified thee; I have appointed thee a prophet unto the nations (Jer. 1:4-5).

For the Son of man shall come in the glory of his Father with his angels; and then shall he render unto every man according to his deeds (Matt. 16:27).

Peter therefore seeing him saith to Jesus, Lord, and what shall this man do? Jesus saith unto him, If I will that he tarry till I come, what is that to thee? follow thou me (John 21:21-22).

So then each one of us shall give account of himself to God (Rom. 14:12).

All too many Christians apparently take it for granted that merely being saved is all that is involved in the Christian life. While according to our understanding of the Word of God, a personal faith in the Lord Jesus

Christ will guarantee one a place in heaven in the hereafter, merely getting to heaven is not enough. For heaven to mean the most to us, we must lay up eternal treasures there in advance of our arrival, and the only way we can accumulate treasures in heaven is by serving God with all our resources while we are on earth. If we wish to be rich in the world to come— find large rewards awaiting us in heaven—we must employ our time, talents, means, energies, personalities, and all else that we possess in the service of God and humanity.

Not only will such wholehearted service to God win for us an eternal reward in heaven; it is the only method by which we can be supremely happy here on the earth.

VIII. Strength for Duties Comes from God

While the Heavenly Father is exacting in his demand that we give him the right of way in our affections and life purposes, he is exceedingly merciful, patient, and gentle; and he makes generous allowances for our human frailties. More encouraging than these things, however, is the fact that our Lord stands ready and willing to supply our every need. Every great servant of God who has followed him completely can testify enthusiastically to his abundant grace, gladly bestowed.

This fact led the great apostle Paul to exclaim exultantly, "I can do all things in him that strengtheneth me" (Phil. 4:13), and "My God shall supply every need of yours according to his riches in glory in Christ Jesus" (Phil. 4:19).

Other Bible encouragement for God's stewards who are considering letting him have his own way in their lives is afforded in the following passages:

My grace is sufficient for thee: for my power is made perfect in weakness (2 Cor. 12:9).

All things are possible to him that believeth (Mark 9:23).

If ye abide in me, and my words abide in you, ask whatsoever ye will, and it shall be done unto you (John 15:7).

I am the vine, ye are the branches: He that abideth in me, and I in him, the same beareth much fruit: for apart from me ye can do nothing (John 15:5).

God not only wants his children to live the happy, abounding life, but also provides the plan and promises us his presence and power as we venture forth in the path of duty. The Lord invites us to follow him, but he does not compel obedience. However, we are losers when we fail to do his bidding.

IX. Stewardship Prepares for Partnership

Countless young men of America who have begun at the very bottom of the ladder in great industrial establishments have risen from one rank to another through the years, by dint of industry, loyalty, and efficiency, until finally they have become partners and officers in their firms.

God takes fuller cognizance of his faithful servants than do the executives of any corporation. He is never slow to appreciate and promote his faithful servants. Those of the Lord's followers who have developed into great stewards he is willing to promote to the high office of partnership in the most exalted of all tasks, the winning of a lost world to a saving knowledge of Jesus Christ.

The rare privileges of partnership are set forth in the following Scripture passages:

Apart from me ye can do nothing (John 15:5).

As thou didst send me into the world, even so sent I them into the world (John 17:18).

If ye abide in me, and my words abide in you, ask whatsoever ye will, and it shall be done unto you (John 15:7).

Abide in me, and I in you. As the branch cannot bear fruit of itself, except it abide in the vine; so neither can ye, except ye abide in me (John 15:4).

He that believeth on me, the works that I do shall he do also; and greater works than these shall he do; because I go unto the Father (John 14:12).

I planted, Apollos watered; but God gave the increase (1 Cor. 3:6).

And working together with him (2 Cor. 6:1).

How much cleaner, happier, and more fruitful our lives would be if they were fully linked up with God! And how far more bountiful our reward in heaven from such a rich partnership!

X. CHRIST NEEDS OUR CO-OPERATION

The world's need, as well as our relationship to God and his abundant rewards for service, should challenge all Christians today to a new loyalty to our Lord.

As was the case when our Saviour was upon the earth, so it is today: "The harvest indeed is plenteous, but the laborers are few. Pray ye therefore the Lord of the harvest, that he send forth laborers into his harvest" (Matt. 9:37-38).

In illustration of the need of more active Christian workers, we need to bear in mind the fact that there are still more than a billion souls in the world who have never yet believed on the name of Jesus Christ. Right in our own Southern Baptist Convention there are 47,872,117 unsaved and unenlisted people (1952). Christ himself taught that "the field is the world," and we have not done our full duty until we have done everything within our power to send the whole gospel to the whole world. If the gospel had been carried to the world earlier, the earth would have been saved from the deplorable predicament in which we find it today. There is no other solvent for personal or social sin.

Our own lives will be greatly enriched, our churches and denomination will be greatly strengthened, millions of immortal souls will be saved from hell, and our Saviour, the Holy Spirit, the Heavenly Father, and all the angels will be made happier in the proportion that we become faithful stewards of God in this highest and holiest of all tasks—winning a lost world to Jesus.

Charles Sumner Hoyt sensed the duties of the church members in this direction when he wrote:

> Is this the time, O Church of Christ! to sound
> Retreat? To arm with weapons cheap and blunt
> The men and women who have borne the brunt
> Of truth's fierce strife, and nobly held their ground?
> Is this the time to halt, when all around
> Horizons lift, new destinies confront,
> Stern duties wait our nation, never wont
> To play the laggard, when God's will was found?
>
> No! rather, strengthen stakes and lengthen cords,
> Enlarge thy plans and gifts, O thou elect,
> And to thy kingdom come for such a time!
> The earth with all its fullness is the Lord's.
> Great things attempt for Him, great things expect,
> Whose love imperial is, whose power sublime.

FOR FURTHER STUDY AND RESEARCH

1. By use of concordance and reference Bible, make a fuller study of Scripture passages dealing with our relation to God as stewards.
2. How many members of your church are faithful stewards of God in the employment of their talents and in giving their means?
3. How much more could your church contribute to the cause of Christ in your community and throughout the world if all the members were faithful stewards?
4. Make a list of local and world conditions which should challenge Christians to a more faithful exercise of their stewardship.

OUTLINE

CHAPTER II

BIBLE'S MESSAGE ON MONEY

...ESTAMENT EMPHASIZES STEWARDSHIP OF POS-...ESSIONS

A careful study of the New Testament will reveal that it has more to say on the stewardship of money or possessions than on any other single subject. Proof of this statement is afforded in the fact that sixteen of Christ's thirty-eight parables—almost half of them—deal with possessions. One verse out of every six in Matthew, Mark, and Luke discusses the right handling of material goods.

The Bible as a whole refers to prayer about five hundred times, to faith fewer than five hundred times, and to material possessions more than a thousand times! Surely if God's Word mentions possessions, or money, more than twice as often as it does such great fundamental subjects as prayer and faith, God did not intend that we should treat the subject of possessions lightly.

While we cannot speak with authority on the motives that actuated the Heavenly Father, we would express in all humility and reverence the belief that God foresaw what a proper conception of the stewardship of possessions would mean in the spiritual development of the Christian and what the co-operation of all his children in the wholehearted practice of stewardship would contribute to the extension of his kingdom in the earth.

Surely God would not have given so great emphasis to any matter that was not of the utmost importance. It certainly behooves his children to give the most earnest study to any topic which God suggests is vital to their welfare.

II. Giving Is Essential to Worship

Few teachings of the Bible on the matter of possessions are clearer and more emphatic than that giving is an essential part of true worship.

This was evidently one idea Christ had in mind when he declared, "Render therefore unto Caesar the things that are Caesar's; and unto God the things that are God's" (Matt. 22:21). Christ meant that giving to God is just as essential a proof of our love to him as is the payment of taxes a proof of loyalty to the state. Moreover, the Lord implied that gifts from God's people are just as essential in promoting his kingdom as are taxes to the support of the government.

However, giving as an act of worship was commanded by God's prophets many hundreds of years before Christ appeared on the earthly stage. Moses, the greatest man of all antiquity and God's chief spokesman in his generation, delivered this charge to his people, "And they shall not appear before Jehovah empty: every man shall give as he is able" (Deut. 16:16-17).

The same idea, phrased in poetic form, was voiced again several hundred years later by David, Israel's sweet singer, in the words,

"Ascribe unto Jehovah the glory due unto his name: Bring an offering, and come into his courts" (Psalm 96:8).

These teachings of Moses and David were in turn supplemented several centuries later by Christ himself, when he said we are under obligation to give of our means and other resources to God in acknowledgment of heaven's blessings upon us: "Freely ye received, freely give" (Matt. 10:8).

But there are reasons other than gratitude and worship why we should give of our means to the Lord, according to the holy Scriptures. The Saviour declared, "The laborer is worthy of his hire" (Luke 10:

7). This general idea was vigorously reinforced by Paul when he wrote, "Know ye not that they that minister about sacred things eat of the things of the temple, and they that wait upon the altar have their portion with the altar? Even so did the Lord ordain that they that proclaim the gospel should live of the gospel" (1 Cor. 9:13-14).

Not only are the pastors and the local work of the churches to be supported by the gifts of the members, but also these contributions should be of sufficient volume to make possible the sending of missionaries to the ends of the earth: "Whosoever shall call upon the name of the Lord shall be saved. How then shall they call on him in whom they have not believed? and how shall they believe in him whom they have not heard? and how shall they hear without a preacher? and how shall they preach, except they be sent? even as it is written, How beautiful are the feet of them that bring glad tidings of good things!" (Rom. 10: 13-15).

The extent to which God's missionary program is dependent upon the practice of genuine Christian stewardship by his people is well stated by Dr. P. E. Burroughs in *Our Lord and Ours*: "Missions must wait upon stewardship. Mission zeal can never go beyond stewardship loyalty. Stewardship is the handmaiden of missions. Mission movements halt because they have not been supported by stewardship teaching and practice. Giving, persistent and perennial giving, must base itself upon stewardship. If the Christian world would produce a generation of givers, the Christian world must first produce a generation of stewards."

Both the need and the significance of a genuine stewardship revival were foreseen by the late Dr. Horace Bushnell, the New England prophet, when he said many years ago, "*One* more revival, *only one more,* is needed—the revival of Christian stewardship, the consecration of the money power to God. When that revival comes, the kingdom of God will come in a day."

All loyal Christians admit the need of such a revival; how can we help to bring it about? We can help, in part, by asking God to help us become wholehearted stewards ourselves, and then by helping, through prayer and personal effort, to enlist many other stewards.

III. GOD'S OWNERSHIP UNDERLIES ALL STEWARDSHIP

Christ assured us that we cannot serve God *and* mammon, but Dr. R. E. Speer points out that the Lord also taught that we can serve God *with* mammon. The moment Christians everywhere come to realize that all they have is God's and that before they spend any of their resources upon themselves they should dedicate a proper proportion of them to the Lord, as a matter of love and appreciation and as a contribution to the furtherance of his kingdom, that moment will we see the Christian cause advance throughout the world as it has never done before.

As was pointed out in the preceding chapter, we are not our own, but are the Lord's, by reason of the fact that he created us in the beginning, redeemed us after we had fallen through sin from our original high estate, and has sustained us by his providential care always. All our faculties and other resources that enable us to accumulate wealth or even make a living are likewise the gifts of God; and the ordinary civilities of life demand that we show our appreciation of the Heavenly Father by returning to him a definite and reasonable proportion of the income he permits us to earn.

However, a dedication of a proportion of our income to God must not be mechanical; it must be prompted by love—such love as will gladly dedicate our means to the Master after we have first given ourselves to him. Some wise steward has said, "God does not get

us until he gets *ours*." In line with this sentiment is
the equally pointed statement, "If your *heart* is on the
altar, your *money* will be there also." Every student
of human nature knows that you can always gauge
the sincerity of a man's interest in anything by the
way he puts his money into it. It is unquestionably
true that the average Christian is a poorer steward of
his means primarily because he is not more interested
in Christ's kingdom.

The placing of money in this world not only deter-
mines where a man's interest lies: his attitude in the
accumulation of money, the saving of money, the investment of money, the spending of money, and the
giving of money also reveals the character of the man.
More than that, these things make the man.

IV. THE TITHE IS THE LOWEST BIBLE STANDARD

While there have been countless discussions regard-
ing the tithe as the proper porportion of a Christian's
income to be dedicated to God, there is one observation on the tenth to which everyone will agree:
namely, that it is the lowest standard of giving recognized anywhere in the Bible.

The late Dr. B. H. Carroll, founder of the Southwestern Baptist Theological Seminary and one of the
greatest Bible scholars Baptists have ever produced,
entertained the correct view of the tithe when he
declared in a sermon many years ago:

It is far from my purpose to make an argument looking to the conclusion that the Mosaic law of the tithe
is binding on the Christian conscience, or is a measure
of Christian obligation. It is not the oldness of the letter, but the newness of the spirit of which I speak. I
would have you see in Christ the body and substance of
all Old Testament shadows. In these shadows were
underlying principles. I would not have you look upon
the tithe as a law in the Jewish sense, for then would
you stop at the law. But, do this much, look at the ex-
pansive income regularly set apart as holy to God which

best enables you to honor God with your substance. Then, as you would not rate yourself a Jew under the law, voluntarily commence with a tenth as a basis— an initial point of departure.

As an adolescent lad, this writer heard his grandfather say he had found out of many years' experience that God could make the nine-tenths of his income, after the first tenth had been dedicated to God, go further and bring larger satisfactions than would the entire income spent wholly for himself and his family. That testimony made a tither of this writer as a boy, and he has found that God has abundantly blessed him through the years in his efforts to honor him with his means and other resources.

Experience and observation have demonstrated that the tither is a happier Christian than the nontither, for he is conscientiously striving to acknowledge the goodness of God and to meet his obligations to a lost world. He gets more joy out of spending what he has left. He is a more useful Christian, for he has a larger share in carrying out Christ's Great Commission. He is a more intelligent Christian, because he seeks to inform himself upon those kingdom causes in which he has made a definite investment. He is a better developed Christian, because his soul has expanded in the proportion that he has invested himself in the Lord's work. He is a richer Christian, because he enjoys a fuller measure of the presence and power of God in his life. And, finally, he will be a far wealthier citizen of heaven, because of the larger treasure he has laid up there through his gifts to the kingdom of Christ on the earth.

If God so graciously blesses those who conscientiously tithe their incomes, why did not Christ issue a definite command for the tithe while he was upon the earth? many sincere inquirers ask. One of the best explanations of that question this writer has seen is

afforded by Dr. Clifton J. Allen of our Baptist Sunday
School Board in his small tract, "A Worthy Financial
Program":

> More important still, if our financial programs are
> to represent obedience to the teachings of the Bible, they
> must ring true to the Bible standard as to the amount.
> Just here it ought to be emphasized that the fundamen-
> tal Bible teaching is God's *ownership* of *all* and man's
> *stewardship* of *all*. But there is a minimum amount
> clearly set forth in the Bible under which no Christian
> dare come. But someone will possibly object and say
> that tithing was a legal requirement of the Old Testa-
> ment law, and that Christians are not under the law
> but under grace. But one is under no less obligation
> under grace than under the law, and tithing is but the
> minimum. Further, tithing was a moral and not a
> ceremonial law. Jesus did not cancel the moral law;
> he confirmed it. He did not destroy it; he defended it.
> He did not tone it down, but up. He did not lower
> the obligations, but heightened them. He did not ask
> for less, but more. He did not abolish tithing, but
> commended it. Tithing is not the *completion* of the
> Christian's duty, but the *beginning*. Tithing is the ex-
> pression of *honesty*, not necessarily *liberality*. Tithing
> is a matter of *minimum obligation*, not necessarily *su-
> preme consecration*.

Persons of large means should certainly go beyond
the tithe in their contributions to the Lord's work.
Millions of persons of modest means find so much joy
in giving the tenth that they go beyond that amount
and experience still larger satisfaction in so doing.

In considering the proportion of his income he should
give to his church, the Christian should make an
intelligent study of where the church money goes and
what it accomplishes, because the steward is under
obligation to invest wisely. Out of every dollar contributed through our co-operating Baptist churches a
part goes to the support of the pastor and other salaried
employees of the congregation; another portion goes

into the teaching and training services of the church, such as the Sunday school and the Training Union; still another portion is applied to the maintenance of the church plant, such as a building fund, repairs, insurance, light, heat, water, janitor's service, and the like; while on the denominational side of the budget supported by the gifts of the members are such items as associational, state, home, and foreign missions, Christian education, ministerial relief, and in many instances our Baptist hospitals and orphanages.

From this it will be seen that the contributor to the church budget has a definite share in the preaching of the gospel and the ministry to the sick and sorrowing at the hands of the pastor. The supporter of the budget helps provide for Bible study in the Sunday school and training in church membership in the Baptist Training Union. He helps to maintain the church equipment and the whole church program in the community, while at the same time he helps to carry forward the whole preaching, teaching, healing, and helping ministry of Jesus Christ in his own state, in our Convention territory, and around the world!

Surely no other money we invest goes into so many, so useful, and so far-reaching channels, and no other investment will bring us so large satisfactions in this world and so large and rich dividends in the world to come.

V. New Testament Prescribes Program for Giving

While there is no question in anyone's mind that the tithe was commanded by Moses in the Old Testament and commended by Christ in the New, the standards of giving in the New Testament are far higher than those set forth in the Old. Let's examine these New Testament standards briefly:

1. Giving is an essential recognition of our debtorship to God—"Freely ye received, freely give" (Matt. 10:8).

2. Giving is better than receiving—"Remember the words of the Lord Jesus, that he himself said, It is more blessed to give than to receive" (Acts 20:35).

3. Giving should be cheerful and should be prompted by love rather than exacted by law—"Let each man do according as he hath purposed in his heart: not grudgingly, or of necessity: for God loveth a cheerful giver" (2 Cor. 9:7).

4. Giving should be liberal—"Give, and it shall be given unto you; good measure, pressed down, shaken together, running over, shall they give into your bosom. For with what measure ye mete it shall be measured to you again" (Luke 6:38).

5. Giving should be both systematic and proportionate—"Upon the first day of the week let each one of you lay by him in store, as he may prosper" (1 Cor. 16:2).

That our Lord himself appreciated and highly commended sacrificial liberality on the part of those who did not limit themselves to the tithe is readily recalled by Bible students from the incident of his anointing at the hands of Mary (Mark 14:3-9) and his comment upon the widow who cast her all into the Temple treasury (Mark 12:41-44).

> Over against the treasury
> He sits who gave Himself for me.
> He sees the coppers that I give
> Who gave His life that I might live.
> He sees the silver I withhold
> Who left for me His throne of gold,
> Who found a manger for His bed,
> Who had nowhere to lay His head;
> He sees the gold I clasp so tight,
> And I am debtor in His sight.
> —Edith B. Gurley

Had all Christ's professed followers through the ages been as faithful in the stewardship of their means and as diligent in personal evangelism as were those at Jerusalem in the first century, the saving message

of salvation undoubtedly would have been carried to
every corner of the earth long, long ago.

VI. ALL OUR RESOURCES SHOULD BE ADMINISTERED FOR GOD

So broad are the New Testament teachings on stewardship of possessions that we have not discharged our
whole duty to God when we have merely placed in his
treasury a dedicated tithe of our income, for this is
only the beginning of our stewardship.   As faithful
stewards we are under obligation to administer the
whole of our possessions in a manner that will be acceptable to God.

The conscientious steward will remember that,
though God permits us to use certain of his resources
while we live, he does not surrender his ownership of
them.   We do not own that which we acquire; for the
resources we employ in our efforts to make money
were contributed mostly by God, though partly by
society.   All the resources of the world were here
when we arrived.   God permits us to use these resources for the season we call life, but he holds us
responsible for the manner in which we employ them
and the manner in which we dispose of the increase
which we accumulate by our activity.   Actually, we
have created nothing.   "We brought nothing into the
world, for neither can we carry anything out" (1 Tim.
6: 7).

VII. COVETOUSNESS IS GREAT FOLLY

Equally emphatic as the Bible's encouragement to
proportionate and liberal giving is its warning against
the selfish accumulation of this world's goods.   So
clear and positive are the Scriptures on this point that
the presentation of a few verses is enough to convince
the sincere Christian of the extreme folly of covetousness:

And he said unto them, Take heed, and keep yourselves from all covetousness: for a man's life consisteth
not in the abundance of the things which he possesseth
(Luke 12:15).

Sell that which ye have, and give alms; make for
yourselves purses which wax not old, a treasure in the
heavens that faileth not, where no thief draweth near,
neither moth destroyeth (Luke 12:33).

But God said unto him, Thou foolish one, this night
is thy soul required of thee; and the things which thou
hast prepared, whose shall they be? So is he that
layeth up treasure for himself, and is not rich toward
God (Luke 12:20-21).

Come now, ye rich, weep and howl for your miseries
that are coming upon you. Your riches are corrupted,
and your garments are moth-eaten. Your gold and
your silver are rusted; and their rust shall be for a
testimony against you, and shall eat your flesh as fire.
Ye have laid up your treasure in the last days. Behold,
the hire of the laborers who mowed your fields, which
is of you kept back by fraud, crieth out: and the cries
of them that reaped have entered into the ears of the
Lord of Sabaoth (James 5:1-4).

For every illegitimate means we employ in accum-
ulating wealth on the earth, in hoarding it after we
have accumulated it, or expending it in extravagant
and riotous or dissolute living, we shall have to give
an account to God in the last day, according to Romans
14:12 and 2 Cor. 5:10.

Nor does the covetous person have to wait until he
enters the other world to begin reaping the rewards
of his grasping disposition, as has been so effectively
suggested by F. H. Boreham in these pointed lines:

Dug from the mountain side, washed in the glen,
Servant am I or the master of men;
Steal me, I curse you;
     Earn me, I bless you;
Grasp me and hoard me, a fiend shall possess you;
Lie for me, die for me;
     Covet me, take me,
Angel or devil, I am what you make me!

One important fact which needs to be borne in mind by all of us is that covetousness, or withholding from the Lord far more than is meet and grasping everything possible, is by no means limited to the rich. While God expects all of us to give to the support of his work, the Scriptures are emphatic in their demand for *proportionate* giving, "Every man shall give as he is able" (Deut. 16:17). The poor man is under just as much obligation to give out of his poverty as the rich man is out of his wealth.

VIII. RICH REWARDS ARE PROMISED LIBERAL GIVERS

And while the Bible pronounces curses and woes upon covetous persons, God promises his richest blessings upon those who are liberal toward him and his cause. God measures liberality not on the basis of the sum given so much as the amount that the giver retains for himself.

Let's look at a few passages from God's Word upon this important principle of stewardship:

> Them that honor me I will honor, and they that despise me shall be lightly esteemed (1 Sam. 2:30).
>
> The liberal soul shall be made fat;
> And he that watereth shall be watered also himself. (Prov. 11:25).
>
> He that hath pity upon the poor lendeth unto Jehovah,
> And his good deed will he pay him again (Prov. 19:17).

But experience, as well as the Scriptures, testifies to the fact that God never allows generous support of his causes to go unrewarded spiritually. During the conduct of the Baptist 75 Million Campaign in the fall of 1919, a very poor widow, operating a very small, rocky, unproductive hillside farm eleven miles from Asheville, North Carolina, heard of this forward movement in her denomination and prayed earnestly that the Lord would make it possible for her to have some share in that effort for the extension of his kingdom.

This dear, good woman, who was helping support a widowed daughter and three grandchildren, had only thirty cents in cash to her name; and the daughter had urged that this sum be used for buying some small Christmas tokens for the children in the home. But as the grandmother prayed she became convinced that it was her duty to give this thirty cents—all the money she had—to the campaign.

On the morning on which this aged widow had planned to drive into Asheville to give her offering to the treasurer of her church, she found that the sole work horse on the farm had a shoulder so sore he could not wear a collar. Not to be deterred from her purpose, the widow decided to walk the entire distance of twenty-two miles into town and back, and that in the rain, that she might be represented in her church's offering to the new program. And she actually trudged the whole distance without so much as a raincoat to protect her, as an old faded shawl was the only thing in the way of a wrap she possessed.

When she reached the treasurer's office and explained her circumstances and her desire, he at first refused to accept the thirty cents, assuring her the Lord would not have her practice such self-denial. But the widow assured him she had made the matter a subject of prayer for many days and that God had told her to give all she had. The treasurer was so rebuked by the widow's generosity that he told the dear woman he would quadruple his pledge; and on that Wednesday night when the officer told the story to the church, many other members greatly increased the amounts they had planned to give.

Soon the news of this sacrificial gift reached the denomination at large and, through the news agencies, the world at large; and several millions of additional money were pledged to the forward movement as a result of this country woman's liberality.

A newspaper syndicate heard of the story and sent one of its best correspondents to North Carolina to find the woman and interview her for a feature article that was sent all over America. The correspondent took a picture of the woman's humble home and family, told her circumstances in detail, and suggested that those feeling disposed to do so might send the woman and members of her family something for Christmas.

In an effort to check up on the responsiveness of the American public, the syndicate sent the same correspondent back to see the widow after Christmas and see what kind of holiday she and her family had enjoyed. The newspaper man found that generous Christmas remembrances had come from all over America and that the dear widow, who had given her all to God, declared the presents had come from God. And had they not done so? The writer is persuaded that when this good saint stands before the judgment bar of God in the last day she will find a far larger blessing is hers than she could ever have anticipated, for she will have a share in all the good that has been accomplished through the years by the additional millions of dollars given to God's cause from the inspiration produced by her giving all she had for the Master.

It is encouraging to note that the Lord has made it possible for each one of us to lay up eternal treasures in the world to come, even though not all of us are permitted to enjoy financial prosperity in this world.

This last statement may be supported amply by a couple of pointed Bible passages:

Lay not up for yourselves treasures upon the earth, where moth and rust consume, and where thieves break through and steal: but lay up for yourselves treasures in heaven, where neither moth nor rust doth consume, and where thieves do not break through nor steal (Matt. 6:19-20).

Charge them that are rich in this present world, that they be not highminded, nor have their hope set on the uncertainty of riches, but on God, who giveth us richly all things to enjoy; that they do good, that they be rich in good works, that they be ready to distribute, willing to communicate; laying up in store for themselves a good foundation against the time to come, that they may lay hold on the life which is life indeed (1 Tim. 6:17-19).

And just as Christ observed and commended the sacrificial gifts of the Jerusalem widow and Mary of Bethany, just so he takes cognizance of all the liberal gifts made by his children today, whether those gifts be of large or small denomination; and he rewards them accordingly.

Our usefulness and happiness in this world, and our joys and rewards in heaven throughout the endless eternity, will be in proportion to our faithfulness as stewards here on earth in the use of all the talents and resources with which God has entrusted us.

FOR FURTHER STUDY AND RESEARCH

1. Make a study of the privileges enjoyed by the Jews in the Old Testament era and compare them with God's blessings upon his children in the Christian dispensation.
2. Take $2057 as the average per capita income of the members of your congregation, multiply this figure by the number of members, calculate a tithe of the total income, and then compare the result with the total sum contributed by your church for all purposes during the past year.
3. Calculate your own or your family's expenditures for all items the past year and then ask yourself how your contributions to religion compare with these other items.
4. How many tithers are there on record in your congregation?
5. Have you ever put God to the test on Malachi 3:10?

OUTLINE

I. NEW TESTAMENT EMPHASIZES STEWARDSHIP OF POSSESSIONS

II. GIVING IS ESSENTIAL TO WORSHIP

III. GOD'S OWNERSHIP UNDERLIES ALL STEWARDSHIP

IV. THE TITHE IS THE LOWEST BIBLE STANDARD

V. NEW TESTAMENT PRESCRIBES PROGRAM FOR GIVING
   1. Giving Recognizes Our Debtorship to God
   2. Giving Is Better than Receiving
   3. Giving Should Be Cheerful
   4. Giving Should Be Liberal
   5. Giving Should Be Systematic and Proportionate

VI. ALL OUR RESOURCES SHOULD BE ADMINISTERED FOR GOD

VII. COVETOUSNESS IS GREAT FOLLY

VIII. RICH REWARDS ARE PROMISED LIBERAL GIVERS

CHAPTER III

THE MOST PRECIOUS THING IN THE WORLD

If someone should ask you what is the most precious thing in the world, what would your answer be? Gold, diamonds, health, character, friends, position, or happiness? Something might be said in behalf of each one of these, of course, but none meets the full specifications embodied in the question. Why?

I. Time Is the Most Precious Thing in the World

If you had $10,000 in gold or a diamond necklace of equal value, and some daring robber should swoop down upon you and snatch your treasure from you, you might succeed in having him caught and your valuables recovered. Or failing in that you might have an opportunity to gain another bag of gold or diamond necklace to replace the one that was stolen.

Health is essential to almost every worth-while achievement in life, but if one's health should be broken temporarily it is generally possible to restore it through proper treatment and sane living.

Character is absolutely fundamental to sound living, of course; but even character, when undermined through moral lapses, may be built up again through grit and the grace of God.

Friends lost may be regained, or new ones may be won to take their places. When one loses a position or when happiness takes wings and flies away, another job or other happiness may usually be found to compensate for that which was lost.

But when time has passed it is gone forever. Neither governmental edict nor God's power can recall it! No wonder the wise Thomas A. Edison was led to observe, "Time is the most important thing in the world." This is true, not only because time that has

[34]

gone can never be redeemed, but also because time, diligently employed, can bring one practically everything else that is worth while in the world.

II. EACH OF US HAS ALL THE TIME THERE IS

One of the gratifying considerations concerning time is that Providence plays no favorites in its distribution, for all of us share it in equal quantities. This is one resource which the wealthy and influential cannot monopolize. All the time there is—every second of every minute of every hour of every day of every month of every year in a whole lifetime is ours to do with as we please, though of course, each one of us will be held accountable to God for the manner in which we employ this most precious of all gifts.

God has given us 24 hours in every day and 8,760 hours in every year. A proper employment of that time, in most instances, can bring us a reasonable supply of this world's goods, health, friends, character, personal culture, advancement in our lifework, a fuller knowledge of God and his will for our lives, opportunities in the service of others, genuine happiness for every day we live, and a chance to lay up rich treasures for the life to come.

III. LIFE IS BRIEF AND UNCERTAIN

The responsibility that is ours in the use of time is emphasized in various passages from the Word of God, which point out that life is brief and uncertain at best:

So teach us to number our days,
That we may get us a heart of wisdom (Psalm 90:12).

Jehovah, make me to know mine end,
And the measure of my days, what it is;
Let me know how frail I am (Psalm 39:4).

Look therefore carefully how ye walk, not as unwise, but as wise; redeeming the time, because the days are evil (Eph. 5:15–16).

Walk in wisdom toward them that are without, redeeming the time (Col. 4:5).

Boast not thyself of tomorrow;

For thou knowest not what a day may bring forth (Prov. 27:1).

But God said unto him, Thou foolish one, this night is thy soul required of thee (Luke 12:20).

We must work the works of him that sent me, while it is day: the night cometh, when no man can work (John 9:4).

Therefore be ye also ready; for in an hour that ye think not the Son of man cometh (Matt. 24:44).

Someone has said, "What we ordinarily call time is only duration. Time in the right sense is duration turned to account."

Of all the tragedies in the average Christian life, probably none is more poignant and few are more inexcusable than that of wasted time. And yet there is probably no sin so generally practiced by people at large—many of them thoroughly decent and respectable persons, too—as that of wasting time.

One of the lamentable aspects of this situation is that the majority of these people apparently are unconscious of their sin. Perhaps they do not realize that they are wasting time. But if one requires two hours for performing a task that could be accomplished in one hour by concentration and enthusiastic application, then one precious hour of sixty golden minutes has been thrown away, and it can never be recalled or in any wise redeemed. If through lack of organizing our work we take three hours in doing a task that might easily have been done in one, then we have thrown away *two* valuable hours we might have employed in some noble service.

And what shall we say of the large volume of precious time most of us throw away attending perfectly inane picture shows, that bring no profit and maybe no injury, other than that they caused us to throw away a lot of the most valuable stuff in the world and with it an opportunity to improve ourselves or bless others. And in the same column that we enter up the loss of the time we throw away at picture shows there should be placed the time wasted in listening to a lot of worthless radio programs, attending a multiplicity of unnecessary parties, riding around in automobiles with nowhere to go and no objective in the riding other than killing time.

In the same category we place the time we have wasted in reading trashy literature; that devoted to perusing many newspapers and magazines in too great detail; musing over fancied wrongs, sighing over the mistakes of the past, worrying over what may happen in the future, sitting around doing nothing at all, running around peddling gossip, or lying in bed for a longer time than is necessary or helpful, especially on Sunday mornings.

If you were to ask the average man to teach a class of boys in the Sunday school, become a department officer, attend a study course, join a group for daily Bible study and prayer, or engage in any similar phase of special service, the chances are he would reply, "I would be glad to, but I simply haven't the time." Yet there isn't one person in ten thousand in America who has his time so fully occupied with essential, constructive duties that he could not consider one more useful line of service. This is true because so many of the activities in which the average church member is engaged today are not essential or even profitable.

Nor are men any greater sinners in killing time than are women. Parties, organizations, committees, shows, and innumerable and inexcusably long telephone conversations drive many high-grade women almost to nervous distraction these days, simply because these women have lost their sense of true values and have allowed themselves to fill their schedules with too many wholly useless things to the exclusion of duties to God and his church.

The time absolutely frittered away in quite non-essential if not definitely harmful activities by countless thousands of adult church members today would be sufficient, if properly conserved, to provide a half hour for Bible study and prayer the first thing each morning; two hours for teachers' meeting and prayer meeting on Wednesday evening; two hours a week more for study of the Sunday school and Training Union lessons; another hour each week for visiting the members of the class and union in their homes or places of business; two hours and a half for Sunday school and preaching services Sunday morning; an hour for the service of others Sunday afternoon; two more hours for the Training Union and preaching services Sunday evening; and a few other hours for emergency duties that might arise during the week. Yes, we can find time for every God-given duty if we will.

O brother man, life's little span will soon be o'er.
  What of the deeds you should have done?
  The victories you should have won?
The day declines, fast sinks the sun to western shore.

That prolific and challenging writer, Dr. Walter B. Pitkin, once made the observation that if we could only tap all the energy in one pound of ordinary matter, such as dirt, iron, coal, wood, ice, or anything else, we could develop therefrom 10,000 horse power for ninety long years! But time, properly employed, is more powerful even than matter.

All the truly great men of the world have been light sleepers and prodigious workers who knew how to utilize their time to the fullest. They have worked long hours and made every moment count for the maximum results. They learned to budget their time even more closely than they did their money, for time is far the more valuable of the two elements.

IV. Time Should Be Budgeted

On a sundial on the campus of All Souls' College at Oxford University there is inscribed this pungent truth, "The hours pass and are laid to our charge." Since time is so valuable, since time lost can never be recaptured, and since someday we shall have to account to God for the manner in which we have employed every precious hour, it behooves each one of us to budget our time carefully and prayerfully in order that none of it be wasted. If we, too, would carefully plan each day, work our plan, and direct our minds to obey our wills, we could literally work miracles in the Master's service.

The eminent author of Ecclesiastes reminded us, "For everything there is a season, and a time for every purpose under heaven" (Eccl. 3:1). The secret of finding the necessary time for every duty lies in successfully budgeting time.

V. Learn How to Plan Each Day

"But how do you go about budgeting your time?" I can hear someone ask. It would be impossible for one to suggest a method of time budgeting that would fit every life, so different are our talents, duties, problems, and situations; but the writer has employed the following plan for a number of years.

1. Before one day is over make a careful outline or summary of the duties of the day to follow, as nearly as they can be anticipated. Estimate as carefully as possible the time necessary for each of these tasks. When the new day arrives undertake to accomplish each task in the time allotted, and when each job has been finished scratch it off the day's program.

2. Learn to concentrate all your resources on the accomplishment of the task in hand. Deafen your ears and close your eyes and mind to every distraction. Do not allow yourself to worry; maintain poise at all

times; and make your mind respond to the dictates of
your will.

3. Get to bed at a reasonable hour each night and
go immediately to sleep. Eat or drink nothing at or
after your evening meal that will interfere with your
sleep; thus you assure yourself a good night's rest.
Get up promptly upon waking and go immediately to
the program of the new day.

4. Start each day aright by devoting a reasonable
period to Bible study and prayer. Many have found
it helpful to refrain from reading the morning newspaper or any other secular matter until they have first
read a chapter from the Word of God and to look into
no human face until they have first communed face to
face with the Heavenly Father. No radio should be
turned on until one has first listened to the voice of
the Lord of the universe as he has engaged in communion with him.

How much time shall one give to his morning Bible
study and prayer? That, too, is a question which no
one can answer for anyone else. Dr. John R. Mott
recommends a minimum of a half hour for every layman, and this writer would commend that suggestion.

The great Baptist minister, Charles Haddon Spur-
geon, one of the busiest men who ever lived, once said
that at the beginning of every average day he spent an
hour in communion with God, but if the day's duties
were unusually heavy and he felt the need of added
strength, he gave two hours to prayer.

It would be sacrilegious to suggest that we pray
from a strictly utilitarian motive; but it is true nevertheless that God honors those servants of his who give
large time to fellowship with him.

Bishop Ralph S. Cushman had this thought in mind
when he penned that beautiful poem he calls "The
Secret":

I met God in the morning
  When my day was at its best,
And his Presence came like sunrise,
  Like a glory in my breast.

All day long the Presence lingered,
  All day long He stayed with me,
And we sailed in perfect calmness
  O'er a very troubled sea.

Other ships were blown and battered,
  Others ships were sore distressed,
But the winds that seemed to drive them
  Brought to us a peace and rest.

Then I thought of other mornings,
  With a keen remorse of mind,
When I too had loosed the moorings,
  With the Presence left behind.

So I think I know the secret,
  Learned from many a troubled way:
You must seek Him in the morning,
  If you want Him through the day.

5. Keep in good physical trim by taking regularly a reasonable amount of physical exercise and mental relaxation.

6. Eliminate from your day's program all non-essential activities. The Christian who becomes the best steward of his time will need to exercise lots of common sense and have the will power to say no to invitations to join unnecessary organizations, serve on nonessential committees, attend useless functions, and engage in unprofitable diversions.

7. Learn to make every moment count. Spare moments, even a few of them at a time, can be utilized in Bible study, reading books for self-improvement, making brief visits to those in need, writing letters of congratulation, encouragement, or condolence, and doing hundreds of other needed things.

Many years ago an ambitious farm lad, anxious to improve every moment along cultural lines, formed the habit of taking a newspaper, magazine, or book with him everywhere he went, so that if an opportunity presented itself at any time to do a bit of helpful reading, he would have the material at hand.

One summer during grain cutting time this farmer boy, whose duty was to shock the grain which his father and older brother were cutting, learned to hurry his shocking so that he might snatch a few minutes occasionally for some extra reading. One day, while waiting for the reaper to get ahead of him a bit, the lad was sitting in the shade of a big shock of grain reading a book when a merchant from the neighboring town rode into the field and saluted the reading youngster thus: "So that's the way you make your living, is it?"

"No," the lad replied; "I work rapidly while I am at it in order to save a little time for learning useful things by reading."

The merchant lived to be past eighty years of age, but was never known beyond two or three counties. The lad, now a man, later worked his way through college, has been listed for several years in *Who's Who in America*, and has friendships and contacts around much of the world. By budgeting his time he is able to serve as a deacon, teach a Sunday school class, attend all the services of his church, visit the sick, do personal soul-winning, and devote several hours a week to community and church work.

There is no more important principle in the conservation and improvement of time than the utilization of the spare moments. Such time has been used by countless persons in acquiring a liberal education and doing a vast amount of work in the service of God and their fellow men.

Another vital consideration in the study of the stewardship of time is that God calls only busy people to tasks of large responsibility, for it is only busy people who have learned the value of time and are thus fitted for the Lord's great tasks.

> Moses was busy with his flocks at Horeb.
> Gideon was busy threshing wheat by the wine press.
> Saul was busy searching for his father's lost beasts.
> Elisha was busy plowing with twelve yoke of oxen.
> David was busy caring for his father's sheep.
> Nehemiah was busy bearing the king's wine-cup.
> Amos was busy following the flock.
> Peter and Andrew were busy casting a net into the sea.
> James and John were busy mending their nets.
> Matthew was busy collecting customs.
> William Carey was busy mending and making shoes.

Then we need to bear in mind that some exceedingly useful lives have been brief ones, so that we are not to concentrate our desires upon living long but living well, especially since none of us knows how long he will be permitted to live.

John Milton in his *Paradise Lost* voiced this sentiment beautifully when he wrote:

> Nor love thy life, nor hate; but what thou liv'st
> Live well; how long or short permit to Heaven.

Another has said, apropos of this general idea, "He who lives long frequently lives too little."

Bill Borden, a young American student who dedicated himself wholly to Christ's service, lived so fully and effectively that by the time he died at twenty-five, he had left an indelible impress for Jesus around the entire world.

VI. Idleness and Laziness Condemned by God

One reason so many people fail to utilize their time properly in the Lord's service, as well as in their own business, is that they are downright lazy and have no desire to work. It will enhance our knowledge of the value of time and effort to review some of the more pointed passages of the Bible in their denunciation of idleness and laziness:

> How long wilt thou sleep, O sluggard?
> When wilt thou arise out of thy sleep?
> Yet a little sleep, a little slumber,
> A little folding of the hands to sleep:
> So shall thy poverty come as a robber,
> And thy want as an armed man (Prov. 6:9-11).
> Slothfulness casteth into a deep sleep;
> And the idle soul shall suffer hunger (Prov. 19:15).

> For the drunkard and the glutton shall come to poverty;
> And drowsiness will clothe a man with rags (Prov. 23:21).

> Why stand ye here all the day idle? (Matt. 20:6).

> And withal they learn also to be idle, going about from house to house; and not only idle, but tattlers also and busybodies, speaking things which they ought not (1 Tim. 5:13).

> If any will not work, neither let him eat (2 Thess. 3:10).

> And I say unto you, that every idle word that men shall speak, they shall give account thereof in the day of judgment (Matt. 12:36).

Since idleness and laziness are vigorously condemned by God, since none of us can possibly know how much time we shall have in which to serve him, and because we are emphatically taught that at the judgment bar we shall have to give an account of our use of our time here on earth, does it not behoove us to consider anew that the only time that we really have at our disposal is NOW?

VII. The Lord's Day Should Be Dedicated to God

Few Bible truths and commands are more frequently ignored by professing Christians than the fact that the Lord's Day should be reserved free for God's worship and service. While the Christian world, under the leadership of the Holy Spirit, substituted the first day of the week for the seventh, by reason of the fact that our Lord rose from the tomb on the first day, we are under as much obligation to keep the first day of the week holy unto God today as were the Jews the seventh day under the Mosaic law.

Notice the directness and positiveness of the Fourth Commandment:

Remember the sabbath day, to keep it holy. Six days shalt thou labor, and do all thy work; but the seventh day is a sabbath unto Jehovah thy God: in it thou shalt not do any work, thou, nor thy son, nor thy daughter, thy man-servant, nor thy maid-servant, nor thy cattle, nor thy stranger that is within thy gates: for in six days Jehovah made heaven and earth, the sea, and all that in them is, and rested the seventh day: wherefore Jehovah blessed the sabbath day, and hallowed it (Ex. 20:8-11).

Ye shall keep the sabbath therefore; for it is holy unto you (Ex. 31:14).

During his public ministry our Saviour powerfully exposed the folly of substituting the letter for the spirit of the law at the hands of the Pharisees, as he showed that it was always in order to serve our fellows in need on the sabbath day; for service to our fellows in the spirit of Christ is service to the Lord himself, who assured us he is the Lord of the sabbath day.

A proper observance of the Lord's Day, however, entails a great deal more than merely desisting from our daily labors. The Bible teaches that a proper recognition of God's claims upon us on the Lord's Day includes gathering at his house for worship, "Not forsaking our own assembling together, as the custom of some is" (Heb. 10:25).

In many of our Southern Baptist churches not half the members attend the morning worship services, and even a smaller proportion of them are present at the

evening hour. It is this writer's conviction that able-
bodied men, women, and young people who are not
providentially hindered from so doing should not only
attend the stated worship services of the church morning and evening, but should also be present at the Sunday school hour for the study of God's Word and at
the Training Union services preceding the evening
worship, for training in Christian service. Mere at-
tendance upon all these stated periods of study, worship, and training will not meet God's approval if it
should degenerate into a mere formality. For our
souls to grow in such activity and for God to be
honored in it, we must worship him in spirit and in
truth.

But after we have done all these things in an acceptable manner, we should use at least a portion of God's
day in honoring him in private Bible study and devotion; serving him along the lines of ministering to the
sick, suffering, and lonely; seeking to win the lost to
the Saviour; and various other forms of service, if we
are faithful stewards of our time and talents.

We have not done our full duty in giving to God a
proper proportion of our time when we have honored
him on the Lord's Day, for all of our time is given us
in trust. A proper recognition of the stewardship of
time will see to it that a period of each day is set apart
for Bible study and communion with the Heavenly
Father. Time will be found for attending the midweek
prayer service of the church; and if one has assumed
any official responsibility in the church, such as serving
as deacon, officer, or teacher in the Sunday school,
W.M.U., or Training Union, he will find time for the
essential daily service that is always entailed in the
faithful performance of the duties of such positions.

Every Christian should bear in mind that there are
168 hours in every week, and it lies within our power,
for the most part, to organize and employ these hours
as we will. By setting aside 56 hours for work and a

similar time for sleep, we still have another 56 hours left for eating, recreation, social contacts, self-culture, and the service of God and our fellows.

The writer repeats, for the sake of emphasis, that every person has all the time he needs for doing everything God would have him do, since each one of us has all the time there is. A careful study of how much time we have at our disposal, a prayer for a revelation from God as to how he would have us invest our time, and a firm resolution that we will conform our expenditures of both time and money to the Lord's will should enable each one of us to invest his time both happily and profitably.

Many of us have read testimonies of the delights and surprises that have come to those who have faithfully tithed their income with the Lord. Equally as large satisfactions and surprises await those who will form an intelligent plan, under God's direction, for the employment of their time and will then follow that plan. Herein lies one of the secrets for the attainment of the abundant, happy, fruitful Christian life.

Paul Laurence Dunbar, the gifted Negro poet, had an excellent conception of the Christian stewardship of time when he penned his beautiful poem, "Too Busy":

The Lord had a job for me, but I had so much to do,
I said, "You get somebody else, or wait till I get through."
I don't know how the Lord came out, but He seemed to get along,
But I felt kind o' sneakin' like—knowed I'd done God wrong.

One day I needed the Lord—needed him right away;
And He never answered me at all, and I could hear Him say,
Down in my accusin' heart: "Nigger, I'se got too much to do;
You get somebody else, or wait till I get through."

Now, when the Lord He have a job for me, I never tries to
shirk;
I drops what I have on hand, and does the good Lord's
work.
And my affairs can run along, or wait till I get through;
Nobody else can do the work that God marked out
for you.

FOR FURTHER STUDY AND RESEARCH

1. Check up on your own use of time by calculating how
many hours a week you give to working, sleeping, eating, recreation, and worship.

2. Remembering there are 168 hours a week, how many
hours have you left after attending to these essentials?

3. What are you doing with the remainder of this time?
Do you find you have any useless activities on your
program, such as suggested in this chapter, which, if
eliminated, would allow larger time for personal culture, personal devotion, and definite Christian service?

4. Do you see anything you can do to promote a wiser use
of time among your friends and in the church services?

OUTLINE

I. TIME IS THE MOST PRECIOUS THING IN THE WORLD
II. EACH OF US HAS ALL THE TIME THERE IS
III. LIFE IS BRIEF AND UNCERTAIN
IV. TIME SHOULD BE BUDGETED
V. LEARN HOW TO PLAN EACH DAY
VI. IDLENESS AND LAZINESS CONDEMNED BY GOD
VII. THE LORD'S DAY SHOULD BE DEDICATED TO GOD

CHAPTER IV

EVERYBODY CAN DO SOMETHING

The writer once served as general superintendent of a large Sunday school, and well does he recall that when he asked the average man to teach a class of boys or young men, serve as department superintendent or secretary, or lead the song service or a devotional exercise, the reply was almost invariably "Oh, I *can't* do *that*." Most of these men had attained some measure of success in their vocations, but they could not trust themselves to do a thing in church work. It is amazing that so many men who are successful farmers, mechanics, lawyers, doctors, merchants, bankers, and teachers, even, feel themselves so incapable of doing any worth-while service along religious lines. Two explanations are readily ascertainable: First, these men lack confidence in themselves because they have never tried; and, second, too many of them allow Satan to whisper into their ears, unconsciously perhaps, "Oh, you cannot possibly do that."

I. Everyone Has Some Talents

1. *God Has a Purpose for Every Life*

For one to say he cannot serve God because he lacks ability is to deny that God created him, for God has a purpose for every life, and the all-wise Heavenly Father could not possibly have brought us into existence for a definite purpose and then have failed to provide us with the talents and resources with which to accomplish that purpose.

It is recognized, of course, that God, in his own wisdom, confers upon some persons much larger endowments than he does upon others; but it must be remembered that God will make much larger demands upon those whom he has so highly endowed than he will upon those to whom he has entrusted smaller talents. But it must be remembered also that Christ assured us that the man of few talents is under just as much obligation to use his small gifts as is the more talented man to employ his larger resources; and the man of small abilities who is faithful in the use of them will receive the same commendation as does the man of large capacities who has likewise been loyal and diligent in his stewardship.

2. *God Has a Place for the Man of Few Talents*

Few stories known to the writer illustrate more effectively how a man of small talents can dedicate them to God and prove of large service to his Master than that of the poorly endowed janitor of a certain small town church.

The pastor of this little church found on very short notice that a very capable evangelist was to pass that way and would spend a night in that city. And although there were no stated services at the church that night, the congregation understood that whenever its members heard the church bell ring late in the afternoon, that signal was to be interpreted as an announcement that special services would be held at the church that night.

Accordingly, when the pastor obtained a promise from the evangelist that he would speak to his congregation on this particular evening, the pastor got in touch with the faithful young janitor and asked him to ring the church bell loud and long.

When the evangelist and pastor reached the church house that evening they found it filled with people. The pastor, proud of his efficient janitor, presented him to the visiting speaker. The latter noticed that the custodian wore on the lapel of his coat a soiled ribbon on which were printed the letters "B.R." As the two ministers walked into the pastor's study for a moment the visitor asked what was the significance of the letters on the soiled ribbon the janitor wore.

"Our janitor likes to be known as the bell ringer of the church, and so proud is he of his humble office that he had that ribbon printed and wears it constantly when he is on duty," the pastor explained. "And the large crowd we have here tonight is due more to the bell ringing of that humble young man than any other factor, I suspect."

"Then I should like to speak with him again after the services are over," the visitor commented.

After the services had been concluded the evangelist shook hands with the custodian and said, "The pastor advises me that the crowd we had tonight was probably due more to your efforts in ringing the bell thoroughly this afternoon than any other thing, and I want to express my appreciation of your good work."

"I was glad to ring the bell, Mister, but that wasn't all I did," the proud man explained.

"Well, that's good; what else did you do?" the evangelist inquired.

"I went by the telephone office and got the operator to call all the people in town and the surrounding territory who have telephones and invite them out to the services tonight," the bell ringer informed the guest.

"Now that was very fine indeed, and I thank you so much," beamed the evangelist.

"But that wasn't all I did," added the janitor.

"Pray tell me what else you found opportunity to do," pleaded the preacher.

"Well, I just walked up and down Main Street speaking to everybody I saw and inviting them out to the services," was the reply.

Here was a man generally regarded as lacking normal intelligence; but he had loyalty, industry, devotion to God's house and cause, and pride in his work; and all these he dedicated fully to the Master's service.

God had great purposes in life for men like Noah, Abraham, Moses, Samuel, David, Daniel, Isaiah, Jeremiah, and other prophets of the Old Testament, as well as John the Baptist, Peter, John, Paul, and others of the New Testament, and countless other great men and women of the centuries that followed; and he endowed them according to the plans he had for them. But God has need for the millions of men of smaller talents, also, and their co-operation in his service is just as essential to the fullest advancement of his kingdom as is the leadership of the leaders.

I believe it was the gifted Josiah Strong who expressed this idea for us admirably when he wrote:

> I thought because I could not teach or preach
>   That God had no engrossing task for me;
> But now I know life cannot reach
>   Beyond His love and man's necessity.
> And so I yield in service all he lends
>   Of time and strength, of money and of skill,
> As one who for a gracious Master spends
>   His bounty in accordance with his will.

3. *We Have a Stewardship of Abilities*

In our study of stewardship heretofore we have given great emphasis to the use of money but have neglected too largely the Bible doctrine of stewardship of talents. Here are a few fundamental considerations to be borne in mind in our study of the stewardship of individual abilities:

(1) *Everybody is somebody.*—Moreover, every individual is important. God places a high estimate upon us as individuals. He knows more about us than we know about ourselves. We are the most important of all God's creatures, having been created in his own image. He loves us with an undying and inexpressible love. He willeth not that any one of us should perish, but that all should come to repentance; and he has even made it possible for us to become joint heirs with Jesus Christ. If God has taken so great interest in us, can any one of us say that he is not important, that there is nothing he can do for God in turn?

(2) *The individual is the unit in every well-organized society,* in the church and in the kingdom of God.

Our Creator, therefore, is looking to each one of us to do his duty as an individual, regardless of the size of his talents and regardless of what others are doing.

(3) *"Each one of us shall give account of himself to God"* (Rom. 14:12).—Just as we are saved as individuals, we shall be rewarded as individuals in the world to come. "He that soweth sparingly shall reap also sparingly; and he that soweth bountifully shall reap also bountifully" (2 Cor. 9:6).

The man of small talents who employs them faithfully and efficiently in the Lord's service will receive the same commendation from the Master in the day of final reckoning as will the faithful servant who has received twice the number of talents that he did (Matt. 25:20-23).

> To each is given a bag of tools,
>   A shapeless mass and a book of rules,
> And each must make, ere life is flown,
>   A stumbling-block or a stepping-stone.
> —R. L. SHARPE

The secret of true stewardship of talents, as is the case with stewardship of every other resource with which Jehovah has entrusted us, is love of and loyalty to God; for when God has gotten *us*, he has gotten *ours*. The secret of the great stewardship of the Macedonian Christians, Paul informs us, was that, "First they gave their own selves to the Lord, and to us through the will of God" (2 Cor. 8:5). That the great apostle had in him much of the spirit of God is evidenced in his declaration to the Macedonian Christians, "For I seek not yours, but you" (2 Cor. 12:14).

II. THERE ARE AMPLE FIELDS OF SERVICE FOR EVERY CHRISTIAN

1. *The Field Is the World; the Harvest Is White*

So broad is God's field (the world) and so abundant and ripe the harvest, that there is urgent need for the labors of every person who has given himself to Christ.

As he was teaching his disciples before his crucifixion, Christ pointed out to them that "The field is the
world" (Matt. 13:38); the fields "are white already unto harvest" (John 4:35), and the situation is such that
many more laborers are needed: "The harvest indeed
is plenteous, but the laborers are few: pray ye therefore the Lord of the harvest, that he send forth laborers
into his harvest" (Luke 10:2).

2. *Abundant Opportunities Confront Adults*

But these principles, sound as they are, are not likely
to grip unenlisted church members unless these truths
are given more concrete and definite application to the
tasks that confront our churches and denomination.
A couple of applications are offered:

One of the greatest needs for personal service in all
of our churches is for more capable and consecrated
men and women to teach boys and girls in the Sunday
school and lead them in the Training Union, particularly those of the Intermediate ages, thirteen to sixteen
years.

According to J. P. Edmunds, statistician of the Baptist Sunday School Board, there are about two million
prospects of Intermediate age for the Baptist Sunday
schools of the Southern Baptist Convention who are
not now in any school. A great host of Intermediate
church members are not in the Training Union.

Think for a moment of the latent power for good or
for evil wrapped up in the lives of two million wide-
awake boys and girls between the ages of thirteen and
sixteen! And unless these boys and girls are con-
tacted before they have passed the Intermediate age,
the chances are strong that they will never be won to
Christ and the church. Figures show that nine persons
out of every ten who become Christians accept the
Saviour before they are seventeen, the age at which
boys and girls pass out of the Intermediate department.
If these two million boys and girls are not reached

and won to the Saviour—if they go out into life and then into eternity unsaved—they will do so largely because of the neglect of Southern Baptists, who have such a preponderance of numbers, organizations, and resources here in our Convention!

And just as the years from nine to sixteen are those in which the majority of Christians have surrendered themselves to the Saviour, this is also the age at which lawlessness usually begins to manifest itself in those who become criminals. If our men and women could be induced to give themselves to the task of winning this vast army of boys and girls to the Sunday school, Christ, and the church, few of them would ever go into crime. Mr. J. Edgar Hoover, head of the Federal Bureau of Investigation, and all other outstanding criminologists of the country agree in their testimony to the effect that it is a very rare thing indeed for a boy or girl actively identified with any Sunday school to fall into the clutches of the law. So in serving Intermediate boys and girls, men and women are not only conserving these young people themselves and enlisting them in the churches and kingdom service, but they are performing also a most valuable social service, in that they prevent many of these youngsters from becoming criminals.

Many of the Intermediates already enlisted in Sunday school, particularly among the boys, drop out because the teachers fail to invest themselves in their work sufficiently to maintain the active interest of the pupils. Many drop out of active church life because of a lack of training in the Training Union. Doing a first class job of teaching or leading Intermediate boys and girls is probably the most difficult task in the whole church category; but, as in every other phase of life, the rewards from such service, when it is faithfully and efficiently done, are correspondingly generous.

Many thousands of thoroughly capable adults have declared they could not possibly teach or lead Intermediates under any circumstances. To such, provided they sincerely wish to be of service somewhere in the church, the writer would commend teaching adults, where the field is several times as large, due to the far larger number of adults who are prospects for Sunday school and church membership.

According to the Baptist Sunday School Board, there are approximately 100,000,000 unreached Adult possibilities for the Sunday schools of the Southern Baptist Convention. There are approximately 3,600,000 members of our own Southern Baptist churches who are not enrolled in any Sunday school, and for every unenlisted church member there are several prospects who are not church members.

These millions of adults, not now in any Sunday school, need to be enlisted in the systematic study of the Bible through the Bible school, not alone for their own sake, but for the sake of their homes, the immediate social circles in which they move, the communities in which they live, and the churches and the kingdom of God.

These adults are needed in the Sunday schools, Training Unions, and churches for the reinforcement they can bring in influence, personal service, and financial support; but the only means of reaching them is through adults who are already enlisted. Young people cannot reach them.

Not all our adult church members can teach the Bible, of course, but all of them have some talents which God and his cause need; and they are under as much obligation to devote to God's service whatever talent they have, whether it be that of singing, giving, soul-winning, ushering, visiting the sick, or what not, as those who can teach are under duty to teach.

Fritz Kreisler, the great violinist, gave this stewardship testimony a few years ago:

I was born with music in my system. It was a gift of God. I did not acquire it. So I do not even deserve thanks for the music. Music is too sacred to be sold, and the outrageous prices charged by the musical celebrities today are truly a crime against society. I never look upon the money I earn as my own. It is public money. It is only a fund intrusted to me for proper disbursement. I am constantly endeavoring to reduce my needs to the minimum. I feel morally guilty in ordering a costly meal, for it deprives someone else of a slice of bread, some child perhaps of a bottle of milk. My beloved wife feels exactly as I do about these things. In all these years of my so-called success in music we have not built a home for ourselves. Between it and us stand all the homeless of the world.

Our churches are full of capable men and women who have not yet become stewards of their talents. Commenting upon this situation Dr. W. B. Hinson once remarked: "The unused ability of the church is the exultation of hell, the surprise of heaven, the loss of man, and the grief of God."

III. EACH MUST DISCOVER AND EMPLOY HIS TALENTS

While God provided each one of us with our peculiar talents to enable us to fulfil whatever mission he has for us, it is incumbent upon us to discover what those talents are and to do our part in the development of those gifts to their highest efficiency.

So emphatic is the Word of God on the necessity of our employing our God-given talents in his service that we quote therefrom more extensively than usual:

1. Not All Have the Same Gifts

And unto one he gave five talents, to another two, to another one; to each according to his several ability (Matt. 25:15).

Howbeit each man hath his own gift from God, one after this manner, and another after that (1 Cor. 7:7).

For even as we have many members in one body, and all the members have not the same office: so we, who are many, are one body in Christ, and severally members one of another (Rom. 12:4-5).

Now there are diversities of gifts, but the same Spirit
(1 Cor. 12:4).

And he gave some to be apostles; and some, prophets;
and some, evangelists; and some, pastors and teachers
(Eph. 4:11).

Also read 1 Corinthians 12:14-30.

2. *It is Our Duty to Discover Our Talents*

Neglect not the gift that is in thee, which was given
thee by prophecy, with the laying on of the hands of the
presbytery (1 Tim. 4:14).

Give diligence to present thyself approved unto God, a
workman that needeth not to be ashamed, handling
aright the word of truth (2 Tim. 2:15).

3. *Having Found Our Talents, We Must Put Them to Work*

And having gifts differing according to the grace that
was given to us, whether prophecy, let us prophesy according to the proportion of our faith; or ministry, let
us give ourselves to our ministry; or he that teacheth,
to his teaching; or he that exhorteth, to his exhorting:
he that giveth, let him do it with liberality; he that
ruleth, with diligence; he that showeth mercy, with
cheerfulness (Rom. 12:6-8).

For which cause I put thee in remembrance that thou
stir up the gift of God, which is in thee (2 Tim. 1:6).

According as each hath received a gift, ministering it
among yourselves, as good stewards of the manifold
grace of God (1 Peter 4:10).

The Adult union is a mighty factor in helping adults
to discover and develop their talents. All adult church
members should be in the Training Union.

IV. EACH ONE MUST RENDER AN ACCOUNT OF HIS STEW-ARDSHIP

Surely this solemn truth cannot be better emphasized than by quoting from God's Word:

So then each one of us shall give account of himself
to God (Rom. 14:12).

For the Son of man shall come in the glory of his Father with his angels; and then shall he render unto every man according to his deeds (Matt. 16:27).

And to whomsoever much is given, of him shall much be required: and to whom they commit much, of him will they ask the more (Luke 12:48).

For whosoever hath, to him shall be given, and he shall have abundance: but whosoever hath not, from him shall be taken away even that which he hath (Matt. 13:12).

And the first came before him, saying, Lord, thy pound hath made ten pounds more. And he said unto him, Well done, thou good servant: because thou wast found faithful in a very little, have thou authority over ten cities. And the second came, saying, Thy pound, Lord, hath made five pounds. And he said unto him also, Be thou also over five cities (Luke 19:16-19).

1. Talents Increase with Use

It is encouraging to observe from life, as well as from the teaching of God's Word, that talents as well as money increase with the using. All of us have observed timid Christians go to work in the Master's service. Then not only did the one talent which they first began to exercise develop with the using, but as they used this one talent the Lord revealed to them that they had others, which they likewise began to employ. The result was that in the course of years these originally timid Christians became outstandingly capable and useful workers in the kingdom.

There was known to the writer a young Texan who was seriously afflicted in his speech. He loved the Lord devotedly and wanted to preach, although this seemed impossible. But the young man became a diligent soul-winner, speaking about this all-important matter to nearly everyone he saw whom he did not know to be a Christian. Although, by reason of his handicaps, this servant of God was never able to leave the parental roof to make his own way in the world, he was so devout and diligent in his efforts to proclaim the Christian message to others that when he died the whole business section of the little town closed for the funeral, and he was given such a tribute of respect as was never accorded any other citizen of that community.

2. *Our Talents Can Be Used Every Day*

There is wide opportunity for the use of our talents in our everyday duties by the attitude we assume toward our work, the manner in which we discharge it, and the faithfulness with which we let our Christian lights shine, even in the humblest walks. Millions of consecrated mothers have shaped the ideals and characters of noble sons and daughters as they went about the high and low tasks of the home from day to day. How much poorer the world would have been had Susanne Wesley, mother of John and Charles Wesley, not been given to the world! How busy a life she lived, ministering to the physical, mental, and spiritual needs of her nineteen children, acting as schoolmistress and tutor to the entire family, and finding time to give stated personal and private religious instruction to each one of those children. That was over 200 years ago, before we had prepared foods available for the table, ready-made clothing, and labor-saving devices in the home!

Almost any of us can accomplish seeming miracles by a proper organization and direction of our time, provided we have the wisdom to choose worth-while activities and the will power to carry out our programs.

V. We Overlook Many Opportunities

1. *Our Boys and Girls Need Enlistment with Training*

While the Sunday school, the Training Union, and the W.M.U. have made marked progress in the enlistment and training of our boys and girls, many of our churches have failed to utilize the services of these young people after they have trained them. As a consequence, many capable young people drop out of the habit of attending the regular worship and prayer services. A wider recognition of the abilities of our boys and girls and the rearrangement of our church programs in such a manner as will enable these young people to be used oftener would go a long way, in this writer's estimation, in supplying our congregations with the trained and enlisted leadership which practically all of them need. Young people are willing and pleased to carry the smallest responsibilities in Christian service when invited to do so, and thus they acquire experience, training, and confidence to assume larger tasks as they become older.

2. We Pass by Small Opportunities While Waiting for Large Ones

On the other hand, too many adults feel it beneath their dignity to perform the smaller tasks, though they would feel highly complimented to be invited to carry the larger responsibilities. Concerning this attitude *The Watchman-Examiner,* New York, some time ago carried the following editorial observation:

> Many Christians are waiting for great opportunities. If these arose they would be found ready with trumpets and drums. Such opportunities rarely come in commonplace lives. Little things well done are what the Lord requires of us. How about last Sunday? Were you at the Sunday school? Were you at the morning and evening service? Did you leave your envelope in the plate? Did you make yourself agreeable to your fellow Christians? Did you give a warm welcome to the visiting stranger?
>
> Do not wait for great opportunities. Do the humble duties of life and do them well.

There are no more naturally capable men and women in America than those who compose the membership of our Southern Baptist churches. Our Baptist constituency is capable of giving a good account of itself in the intellectual, social, economic, political, and professional ranks of all our states. Our pastors are outstanding in their field.

But too few of our more capable men and women, comparatively speaking, have fully dedicated their talents and other resources to the service of the Saviour. In all our churches we need to give earnest, prayerful consideration to the matter of enlisting all our people, the highly capable as well as those of only moderate and mediocre natural gifts, along the lines of evangelism, stewardship, personal work, or in whatever other field their talents can be utilized.

3. *Christ Wants Our Best*

We have large numbers; we have the money; we have ability; but so far we lack the vision, the loyalty, the love, and the will to put Christ and the kingdom first in our thinking, prayers, gifts, and efforts. Nothing less than the best is worthy of our Lord, who forsook his throne in heaven and came down to earth, where he took on the form of flesh, assumed the role of a servant, suffered hardships, indignities, and persecution such as no one else ever bore, all because he loved us and wished to redeem us. Surely the very best of each one of his redeemed children is not too much for him to ask of us today! We as individuals can make a start in this direction by first giving the Lord our best and then seeking to enlist others in joining us in this high adventure.

God wants our best. He in the far-off ages
   Once claimed the firstling of the flock, the finest of
      the wheat;
And still He asks His own, with gentlest pleading,
   To lay their highest hopes and brightest talents at
      His feet.
He'll not forget the feeblest service, humblest love;
   He only asks that of our store, we give the best we
      have.

Christ gives the best. He takes the hearts we offer
    And fills them with His glorious beauty, joy and peace,
And in His service as we're growing stronger
    The calls to grand achievements e'er increase.
The richest gifts for us, on earth or in heaven above,
    Are hid in Christ. In Jesus we receive the best we
    have.

And is our best too much? dear friends, we should re-
    member
    How much our Lord poured out His soul for us,
And in the prime of His mysterious manhood
    Gave up His precious life upon the cross.
The Lord of lords by whom the worlds were made,
    Through bitter grief and tears, gave us the best He
    had.

—ANONYMOUS

FOR FURTHER STUDY AND RESEARCH

1. Get your Bible and make a special study of the number of individuals whom God called to special tasks,
such as Abraham, Moses, Joshua, and Samuel.

2. Take a half hour for prayerful reflection and endeav-
or to list all the special talents for Christian service
God has given you. How many of them are you using?

3. Make a study of the needs of your church in additional
workers from among the men, women, and young people of your congregation. Then ask God to show you
the persons who possess the qualifications needed and
begin praying that God will open the eyes of these
persons that they may see their opportunity.

4. Then go to the pastor, Sunday school superintendent,
Training Union director, or other workers in need of
assistants and propose the names of the persons on
your list.

5. Form the habit of commending new workers in your
church when their service merits it.

OUTLINE

I. EVERYONE HAS SOME TALENTS
  1. God Has a Purpose for Every Life
  2. God Has a Place for the Man of Few Talents
  3. We Have a Stewardship of Abilities

II. THERE ARE AMPLE FIELDS OF SERVICE FOR EVERY CHRISTIAN
  1. The Field Is the World; the Harvest Is White
  2. Abundant Opportunities Confront Adults

III. EACH MUST DISCOVER AND EMPLOY HIS TALENTS
  1. Not All Have the Same Gifts
  2. It Is Our Duty to Discover Our Talents
  3. Having Found Our Talents, We Must Put Them to Work

IV. EACH ONE MUST RENDER AN ACCOUNT OF HIS STEWARDSHIP
  1. Talents Increase with Use
  2. Our Talents Can Be Used Every Day

V. WE OVERLOOK MANY OPPORTUNITIES
  1. Our Boys and Girls Need Enlistment with Training
  2. We Pass by Small Opportunities While Waiting for Large Ones
  3. Christ Wants Our Best

CHAPTER V

CANDLE OR SEARCHLIGHT

Mounted on a steel tower, 135 feet above the roof of the skyscraper Palmolive Building in Chicago, is the two billion candle power searchlight known as the Lindbergh Light, which throws its beams across twelve states and hundreds of miles into the Dominion of Canada. Cities as remote as Buffalo, New York City, Memphis, and Omaha fall within the radius of this mighty beacon. A half-dozen such powerful searchlights, it has been estimated, would illumine the whole United States.

We properly hail this contribution of men of science and business to safety in air travel and commerce. Men of religion should put the same deep thought, courageous initiative, and loyal devotion into lighting the world with the light of the gospel, which drives away the darkness of sin. When, in the nearly two thousand years since Christ delivered the Great Commission to his disciples, has the world needed the penetrating light of the gospel more than it does today? The hatred, the oppression of minorities, the poverty, the prevalence of war with its attendant evils of cruelty, disease, want, and immorality, and the general denial of God that exist in so much of the globe today, could not have come into being had the world been fully penetrated by this most wholesome light in all the universe.

Fortunately, it is possible in God's economy for this gospel light to be shed abroad in every individual heart. It lies within the power of those of us who possess this light to create a desire for it on the part of others by keeping our lamps so well trimmed and nourished that they will radiate their brightest light and nurturing warmth. There is a sufficient number of professing Christians in almost every section of the

[65]

world today for the whole earth to be illumined by the
light of Christ if every individual Christian would only
let his light shine as he should.

This brings us to a study of that large body of Bible
teaching upon the stewardship of influence and example. We shall have gone a long way toward bringing the remainder of the world to an acknowledgment
of Christ as Lord when all his professed followers let
their lights shine by exerting a definite Christian influence in the various circles—domestic, social, business, professional, political, and religious—in which
they move.

I. Everybody Wields Some Influence

1. *None Liveth or Dieth to Himself*

Fundamental to the study of the Bible's message
on the stewardship of influence is the fact that every
individual in the world wields some influence. "None
of us liveth to himself, and none dieth to himself"
(Rom. 14:7) is the Bible authority upon that point;
and that simple, emphatic declaration from the Word
of God needs no further support.

2. *Silent Life of Humblest Saint Counts for God*

The silent testimony of a consecrated Christian life
has frequently proved a more effective witness to the
power of God in regenerating the soul than the most
eloquent sermon. On the other hand, the ineffective
living of millions of professing Christians has been
used of Satan to turn other millions of non-Christians
against religion.

II. Christians Must Set High Standards of Conduct

1. *Christian Life Is a Transformed Life*

While Christ warned us against the sin of judging
others no one will deny that multitudes of us who have
taken on the name of Christ have failed to grow in
Christlikeness. The Christian life, in its true sense,

is a transformed life, one that is so different from the life of the world that the non-Christian can recognize the genuine Christian more readily by the example he sets and the influence he wields than by the professions he utters. If a professing Christian lives no higher type of life than do the worldly persons with whom he associates, he has given no evidence of the fact that he has been born again.

2. *World Expects Christians to Live Separated Life*

"Come ye out from among them, and be ye separate, saith the Lord" (2 Cor. 6:17) is God's command to all of us who have accepted Christ as Saviour; and the loyal child of God will seek with all sincerity and earnestness to heed that order. What does compliance with this ultimatum from the Lord mean? It means that we are no longer our own, "having been bought with a price," and that our example in every activity in which we engage should be such as will please and glorify him who has redeemed us.

A young woman, an active member of a church, became infatuated with dancing. Wishing to have the counsel of her pastor on the matter, she asked him if it would be right for her to attend a dance.

"Do you think you could speak to a lost soul about the Saviour at the dance?" the pastor inquired.

"I believe I could," was the young woman's reply.

"Well, that has been the test I have always applied to places of amusement or activities about which questions have arisen in my mind," the pastor commented.

The young woman decided to attend the dance, and while she was dancing with a young man that evening she inquired of him, "Are you a Christian?"

"No," he replied promptly, "Are you?"

"Yes," came the prompt response.

"Then what are you doing here?" he demanded.

The life of every church in America will be transformed when all its members come to comprehend the significance of Christ's command for them to come out from the world and be separate in their ideals and conduct. Such Christians will, of course, follow the example of the Saviour in making friends of publicans and sinners to win them also to the Lord.

Paul's ideal for the attitude and conduct of the Christian, "Our old man was crucified with him, that the body of sin might be done away, that so we should no longer be in bondage to sin" (Rom. 6:6), should be the ideal which the churches demand of their members today. A generation or so ago many of our churches were probably too rigid in their discipline, or at least a bit too ruthless in administering it, particularly in regard to the young people of the congregations. Mere rumors that certain young church members had been seen at a dance were seized upon by some churches as an occasion for expunging the names of those young people from the rolls, without verifying the rumors or giving the erring young people an opportunity to confess their sins and be restored to the fellowship of the churches.

Today, however, the pendulum has swung quite as far in the opposite direction and church discipline has become a lost art. The writer is not pleading for the mechanical revision of the church rolls through the medium of discipline so much as he is urging that every church member make a careful study of the Bible message on Christian conduct and revise his own behavior in accordance with the Bible standards.

3. God Provides Needed Grace

Every professing Christian should heed the earnest injunction of Paul, "Abstain from every form of evil" (1 Thess. 5:22). That high ideal is difficult to attain, but it is not impossible, for as the Saviour himself reminded us, "All things are possible to him that believeth" (Mark 9:23). Paul likewise encouraged us in striving for high objectives in the Christian life when he assured us, "I can do all things in him that strengtheneth me. . . . And my God shall supply every need of yours according to his riches in glory in Christ Jesus" (Phil. 4:13, 19). So while God is making high demands upon us in the matter of our Christian influence, he is also supplying us with the means whereby we may be able to measure up to those worthy goals.

III. Christians Must Consider Others in Determining Their Conduct

1. *"Ye Are the Light of the World"*

God gives us another challenge to set a high standard in our Christian influence by urging that we consider the welfare of others weaker than ourselves in determining what courses we shall pursue.

"Ye are the light of the world. A city set on a hill cannot be hid. . . . Even so let your light shine before men; that they may see your good works, and glorify your Father who is in heaven" (Matt. 5:14-16).

These words from Christ himself show how he has honored us by making us his representatives on the earth so that others can see him through us; and if we allow our Lord to be seen in us unmistakably, then others will turn to God and glorify him.

2. *Adults Should Be Examples to Young People*

Professing Christians need to be careful of their example and influence not only because their conduct may affect the unsaved, but also to set an example that will be helpful to young Christians. Our Lord also anticipated this need when he warned us in this very vigorous statement: "Whoso shall cause one of these little ones that believe on me to stumble, it is profitable for him that a great millstone should be hanged about his neck, and that he should be sunk in the depth of the sea" (Matt. 18:6).

If every deacon, every Sunday school teacher, and everyone else who occupies a position of leadership in our churches could once catch the full implications of this message from the Lord, what a transformation it would work in their lives and their usefulness in Christian service! And *every* adult Christian, as well as those who lead in the churches, needs to ponder anew, in the light of the Saviour's warning, the tremendous responsibility that is ours in watching our conduct before young people.

3. *Self-Denial for Sake of Others Helps All*

There is an adage in our American political philosophy to the effect that though this is a free country, our liberty ends where the other fellows nose begins. It should be remembered, however, that that high principle was embodied in the Bible centuries before America had ever been discovered. Paul, the greatest of all Christ's followers, expressed our obligation to shape our own conduct in the light of the welfare of others when he wrote: "It is good not to eat flesh, nor to drink wine, nor to do anything whereby thy brother stumbleth. . . . Now we that are strong ought to bear the infirmities of the weak, and not to please ourselves" (Rom. 14:21; 15:1).

Just as we never know the highest joys in Christian giving until we have learned to give sacrificially, just so we shall never know the highest satisfactions in Christian living until we have learned to deny ourselves in our conduct for the sake of others.

Probably the most radiant young Christian this writer ever knew was a fifteen-year-old Chinese lad, who came to this country a few years ago to study the English language. He could not speak a word of English when he came. He was enlisted in a Baptist Sunday school where he accepted Christ and united with the church. He gave thirty minutes each day to earnest Bible study, gave the first period of each day to prayer, organized his time so that not a moment of any day would be wasted, and undertook with God's help so to regulate his every word, act, and attitude that it would help him wield a helpful Christian influence upon all with whom he came in contact. He undertook to go to no place where he believed a Christian ought not to go, and he endeavored to win to Christ the unsaved American boys with whom he came in contact at high school. His plan was to become a doctor and then return to China as a medical missionary. This young Chinese Christian, only in his middle teens, had already learned the stewardship of example, the stewardship of time, and the stewardship of prayer! What could we native American Christians do in these directions if we tried!

But let us bear in mind the fact that the influence our example has on others has a positive as well as a negative implication, as pointed out by Paul in 1 Tim. 4:12: "But be thou an ensample to them that believe."

An interesting illustration of how the First Baptist Church, Abilene, Texas, undertakes to enlist members of its official family in becoming examples to others in both conduct and service was reported some years ago through the Baptist Sunday School Board as follows:

"Read this statement, will you?

"The First Baptist Church, Abilene, Texas, Dr. Millard Jenkins, pastor, has in its Sunday school 454 teachers and officers, including class officers.

"No teacher or officer plays cards or dances.

"During one year 50,175 visits have been made; 35,000 cards and letters have been sent; and 17,000 phone calls have been given in the interest of the school."

IV. CHRISTIANS SHOULD PLEASE GOD IN THEIR INFLUENCE

1. *God Has First Claim upon Us*

But challenging as are the various messages from God's Word exhorting us to do nothing that would cause others to stumble and commanding us to be examples to everybody else, even more convincing to the loyal child of God should be those passages to the effect that the honor and glory of the Lord should be the primary motive in all our conduct.

"No soldier on service entangleth himself in the affairs of this life; and he may please him who enrolled him as a soldier" (2 Tim. 2:4). This was the figure of speech Paul employed in driving home the lesson that those of us who have enlisted in the service of King Immanuel should not entangle ourselves in worldly matters, but give ourselves wholeheartedly to the service of our Lord, who has not hired us as warriors of old used to hire their soldiers, but who actually bought us with his own precious blood.

"And he died for all, that they that live should no longer live unto themselves, but unto him who for their sakes died and rose again" (2 Cor. 5:15).

2. *"Do All to the Glory of God"*

In his desire to make the high duty and privilege of those who have accepted Christ even clearer to those who would know the fullest joys of the Christian life, Paul exhorted them after this fashion: "Whether therefore ye eat, or drink, or whatsoever ye do, do all to the glory of God" (1 Cor. 10:31). It was living up to this high ideal in its entirety that enabled Paul to become the most useful and the happiest follower the Lord Jesus ever had.

Do we as Christians really want to live the highest type of life, or do we want to reap the pleasures of the world on the one hand and pluck just enough fruit from religion to keep our souls from absolute starvation? Someone has said that all too many Christians apparently want just enough religion to get them into heaven and just enough to keep them out of hell. Isn't that true of many you know?

This study is aimed to point the way to the higher type of Christian life, where the individual wishes to rise above the world, not for his own sake alone, but that he may thereby honor the name of his Redeemer and at the same time point others to the Lamb of God, that takes away the sin of the world and redeems the life as well as the soul of the one who puts his trust in him.

3. *Perfection Is the Ultimate Aim*

For the individual who is aspiring to this loftier life the Bible gives explicit directions. That one must so plan his ideals and service "that in all things he [Christ] might have the pre-eminence" (Col. 1:18).

"But how can we so live that in all things Christ might have the pre-eminence?" one may properly ask. We shall let the Bible answer this query. The first step in that growth in grace is set forth thus: "For hereunto were ye called: because Christ also suffered for you, leaving you an example, that ye should follow his steps" (1 Peter 2:21). If one sincerely wants to follow in the steps of the Saviour, he will count it a privilege to deny himself ease, pleasures, and everything else that would be contrary to Christ's will and to engage in whatever service the Master might have in mind for him.

Paul attained to this wholehearted surrender to the will of God, for he was able to declare, "For to me to live is Christ" (Phil. 1:21).

But one greater than Paul gave specific instruction as to the type of influence his followers should seek to exert when he exhorted them in the Sermon on the Mount: "Ye therefore shall be perfect, as your heavenly Father is perfect" (Matt. 5:48). We do not understand that our Lord demanded absolute perfection of his followers here on earth; but he is pleased when his followers long for perfection and strive for it daily, by watchfulness, Bible study, prayer, and wholehearted service.

The path of Christian duty necessarily entails a lot of self-denials and hardships of a type, but the thoughtful Christian will remember that our Lord is not only just but generous, and that for every self-denial we undergo for his sake he repays us with satisfactions innumerable which the world cannot appreciate or even understand.

Ella Wheeler Wilcox had something of this thought in mind many years ago when she penned these challenging lines:

> We turn our sad, reluctant gaze
> Upon the path of duty;
> Its barren, uninviting ways
> Are void of bloom and beauty.
> Though often dreary, dark, and cold
> It seems as we begin it,
> As we press on, lo, we behold
> There's heaven in it.

V. CHRISTIANS MUST GIVE AN ACCOUNT OF THEIR INFLUENCE

1. *Our Accounting Must Be Made Individually*

The Bible's message upon the fact that on the final day of judgment each one of us will have to give an account for all the deeds done in the body is so plain, pointed, and emphatic that it is really amazing that so few Christians, apparently, give the heed to it that they should.

Let us look at three brief Bible passages upon this point:

So then each one of us shall give account of himself to God (Rom. 14:12).

And I say unto you, that every idle word that men shall speak, they shall give account thereof in the day of judgment (Matt. 12:36).

For the Son of man shall come in the glory of his Father with his angels; and then shall he render unto every man according to his deeds (Matt. 16:27).

2. *Christ Will Judge Both Our Words and Deeds*

What specific instructions do these vital messages for the Word of God have for us, his children? Here are a few important ones which we gather at a glance from the passages cited:

(1) *Each one* of us will be called upon to give an account at the last day. *None* of us can possibly escape the eye or the record of Almighty God.

(2) We will have to give an account of ourselves. It will not be ours to account for the shortcomings of the pastor, the deacons, the Sunday school officers and teachers, the leaders in the Training Union, the W.M.U., and the Brotherhood, or even our denominational leaders or our neighbors. Our responsibility will be limited to ourselves, save as our influence has affected others for good or evil.

(3) Our *words* as well as our *deeds* will have to be accounted for, and our *idleness* as well as our *activities*. Has it ever occurred to you how large foolish talk looms in the eyes of God?

(4) Though all of us who get to heaven will go there through our personal faith in the merits of the Lord Jesus Christ, our Lord himself, who will be the supreme and only judge on the last day, assures us that we will be rewarded according to our deeds here on the earth. The individual who has served the Saviour in this life to the best of his ability will find a large reward awaiting him in heaven, whereas the one who has merely given his heart to Christ, but has withheld his life and service, will manage to get into heaven on the last day, but will find that he has done nothing to earn a reward to enjoy throughout eternity.

3. *Souls May Be Saved, When Works Are Destroyed*

This point is brought out more fully and emphatically by Paul in his letter to the church at Corinth: "According to the grace of God which was given unto me, as a wise masterbuilder I laid a foundation; and another buildeth thereon. But let each man take heed how he buildeth thereon. For other foundation can no man lay than that which is laid, which is Jesus

Christ. But if any man buildeth on the foundation gold, silver, costly stones, wood, hay, stubble; each man's work shall be made manifest: for the day shall declare it, because it is revealed in fire; and the fire itself shall prove each man's work of what sort it is. If any man's work shall abide which he built thereon, he shall receive a reward. If any man's work shall be burned, he shall suffer loss: but he himself shall be saved; yet so as through fire" (1 Cor. 3: 10-15).

What then will our record be in that final day? It will be just what we ourselves care to make it while we are still in the flesh. If we live lives that are above reproach, striving to please God in all that we do and honoring him faithfully in the employment of all the resources with which he has entrusted us, then we will have no embarrassing moments to confront at the judgment bar. Instead we will be gladly greeted by the Lord with some such salutation as, "Well done, good and faithful servant: . . . enter thou into the joy of thy Lord."

But what will be the feeling of that vast army of unenlisted Christians when they go up to meet the Master face to face, and are confronted by him with the record that they refused to take up their cross and follow the Lord as he commanded? They will be reminded that they frequently cut the Sunday worship in order to attend picnics, go on Sunday excursions or joy rides, or maybe just to spend the whole of the Lord's Day in unnecessary visiting of relatives and friends. Many church members patronize such secular amusements as Sunday picture shows, ball games, and the like. Other church members have no scruples about attending or even giving parties on prayer meeting nights, and in more recent years Sunday parties are given by some. Millions of church members play golf on Sunday, bet on ball games, horse races, golf, or political elections. Others still play cards for prizes, either dance themselves, or give dances in their homes. Some church members today even take intoxicating drinks at social functions, rather than run the risk of being called old-fashioned, straight-laced, puritanical, or even peculiar, and indulge in what many have termed "polite" swearing, when of course there is no such thing.

How are these persons going to account to the Lord for the fact that their influence on others has been for evil rather than for good? Just how much will heaven mean to them, if they have no reward laid up for them there? Hundreds of millions of Christians will be called to account for their failure to set a good example in giving of their means to God's causes and in personal soul-winning.

4. *The Victorious Life Is Not Impossible*

But there is no need of our living barren lives. Every day offers us opportunities for high thinking, noble living, and helpful service. The busy housewife at her duties about the home, the busy teacher in the school-room, the carpenter plying his tools, the salesman in his frequent contacts with the public, the farmer as he tills the soil, the lawyer as he represents his clients at the bar, the physician as he ministers to the physical ills of humanity, the editor as he prepares the news or editorials for the consumption of the busy public, and everybody else under the sun has an opportunity to let his light shine for the Saviour wherever he goes, and to serve needy, sin-sick humanity on every hand.

Living the superior life is not an easy task, but neither is anything else that is worth while. But the life whose influence is altogether for the noblest and the best is far from impossible. Maeterlinck said, "If a bee gets very far from the hive it perishes." Christ declared, "As the branch cannot bear fruit of itself, except it abide in the vine; so neither can ye, except ye abide in me. . . . He that abideth in me, and I in him, the same beareth much fruit: for apart from me ye can do nothing" (John 15:4-5).

There are those, however, who say it is impossible to abide in Christ, since the world is so full of temptations of every character. There is a lesson for these in the well-known story of a noted aviator bound from London for India, who, while high above the earth over the Arabian desert, suddenly detected the gnawing of a big rat on one of the most delicate bits of mechanism of his plane. It was hundreds of miles to the next landing field, and as he could never have taken to the air again from the desert, had he landed in order to kill the rodent, he was perplexed for a moment as to how he was to avert a catastrophe. Then suddenly he recalled that rodents could not live in a high altitude, so he pointed his plane upward into the rarer atmosphere and in an unbelievably short time the gnawing ceased, for the rat had died. Sins cannot exist in a life that dwells in the presence of the Saviour.

We all have been inspired by the high purity of the great characters of the Bible, such as Enoch, who walked daily with God and pleased him; Abraham, known as the friend of God; Moses, God's great lawgiver, who chose to suffer ill treatment with the people of God rather than to enjoy the fruits of sin for a season; Joshua and Caleb, the faithful, famous spies who sought to challenge the Israelites to go up in faith to possess the Promised Land; Joseph, who steadfastly refused to do evil under the most enticing circumstances; Shadrach, Meshach, and Abednego, who refused to bow the knee to the golden image when failure to do so was punishable with death; and John the Baptist, who denounced a king for his adultery, and paid with his life for his loyalty to his convictions!

The whole world for all time has been enriched by the purity and courage of these noble servants of God. Although none of us enjoys so large opportunities for letting our lights shine as were vouchsafed to these Christian patriarchs, and there is no other sacred record to be published that will perpetuate our deeds of devotion, our influence is considerable nevertheless. It has been said that each one of us is probably the best Christian somebody knows. What estimate of religion have these unconverted friends of ours who are reading our lives from day to day and are looking to our example for guidance? Will we stand approved or condemned in the last day, on the basis of the manner in which we have let our lights shine?

Upon the truth of the scriptural declaration that "Ye are an epistle of Christ," J. Phil Appel has written that well-known poem entitled "The Gospel According to You," which is given here as the closing meditation for this chapter:

"The epistle of Christ," saith the Spirit, "are ye."
  But we are not written with ink that will fade,
Not in tables of stone, but in hearts that are flesh
  Has our Master's inscription been lovingly made.

He lived and he died. He arose from the dead
  And returned to the Father to bless on and on;
And men read and are saved by the gospel of grace
  Penned according to Matthew and Mark, Luke and John.

Blessed Lord Jesus Christ, make my life wholly thine,
  An epistle for all who thy Word do not see,
And who never will read Matthew, Mark, Luke, and John,
  But who will read the story according to me.

But not all are epistles of Jesus our Lord.
  Satan, too, uses lives that his story will tell;
Vile epistles beguiling to innocent hearts,
  Leading them on the road that goes down into hell.

If you are an epistle indited by Christ,
  All your thoughts, words, and deeds will ring true;
Then lost souls will be saved as they ponder and read
  Ev'ry word of the gospel according to you.

As you carry your letter through life day by day,
  Oh, take care that the writing is Christ's, and thus true
For the souls who'll not read Matthew, Mark, Luke, and
    John,
  But who'll have to accept it according to you.

Your epistle, my friend, is the life you lead,
  Is it false and misleading, or honest and true?
Stop and think! It means heaven or hell to the souls
  Who read only the gospel according to you.

FOR FURTHER STUDY AND RESEARCH

1. By aid of your concordance and parallel reference Bible, make a daily devotional study for a week of the demands the Word of God makes upon Christians in living a superior life.
2. Who wielded the most positive Christian influence you ever felt?
3. What six members of your church wield the most helpful influences along spiritual lines, and why?
4. Ask God to help you examine your own conduct and determine whether it is helping anybody or hurting anybody, and to what extent. Can your influence be neutral?
5. Taking the members of your church as a whole, is their conduct so superior to that of worldly people as to make their influence count positively for Christ?

OUTLINE

I. EVERYBODY WIELDS SOME INFLUENCE
  1. None Liveth or Dieth to Himself
  2. Silent Life of Humblest Saint Counts for God
II. CHRISTIANS MUST SET HIGH STANDARDS OF CONDUCT
  1. Christian Life Is a Transformed Life
  2. World Expects Christians to Live Separated Life
  3. God Provides Needed Grace
III. CHRISTIANS MUST CONSIDER OTHERS IN DETERMINING THEIR CONDUCT
  1. "Ye Are the Light of the World"
  2. Adults Should Be Examples to Young People
  3. Self-Denial for Sake of Others Helps All
IV. CHRISTIANS SHOULD PLEASE GOD IN THEIR INFLUENCE
  1. God Has First Claim upon Us
  2. "Do All to the Glory of God"
  3. Perfection Is the Ultimate Aim
V. CHRISTIANS MUST GIVE AN ACCOUNT OF THEIR INFLUENCE
  1. Our Accounting Must Be Made Individually
  2. Christ Will Judge Both Our Words and Deeds
  3. Souls May Be Saved, When Works Are Destroyed
  4. The Victorious Life Is Not Impossible

CHAPTER VI

THE MOST IMPORTANT WORK IN THE WORLD

I. WHY ARE WE NOT SOUL-WINNERS?

Did you ever make a survey of your congregation to ascertain how many members really make any serious effort to win others to Christ?

Comparing the number of additions to all our Southern Baptist churches by baptism each year with the combined membership of the churches affiliated with the Southern Baptist Convention, we find the ratio ranges from one to twenty to one to twenty-three, according to whether the additions upon profession of faith have been larger or smaller than usual for a given year.

Since there are in some of our churches a few workers who win numerous others during the year, and many of the professions are due to the labors of pastors and evangelists, the actual number of soul-winners is far fewer than one out of every twenty church members.

Every Christian who has ever engaged in it will testify that winning souls brings larger satisfactions to the worker than any other phase of service on earth. The Bible also reveals that the rewards for soul-winning in the world to come will be larger than those for any other phase of Christian effort in which we can engage.

Why, then, do so few Christians, comparatively, engage in this highest of all forms of Christian service? The whole answer would involve a number of different factors, of course, but a few of the reasons which lie on the surface are presented briefly:

1. *Too Little Emphasis Given to Soul-Winning*

All too little emphasis upon this phase of service has been given in the churches, with the result that very few Christians feel any definite responsibility for the salvation of the lost.

2. *Average Church Member Unprepared for the Task*

The average church member, when he does consider the matter, feels wholly unprepared for the task of soul-winning. He does not know how to make the contact nor how to proceed after the interview with the prospect has been obtained.

3. *Our Example Nullifies Our Influence*

It is the common excuse of many who are invited to engage in personal evangelism that their own lives present such a poor practice of religion that they are ashamed to ask an unsaved person to give himself to the Saviour.

4. *We Have Little Compassion for the Lost*

All too few church members apparently have any compassion for the lost.

But no matter what our record in soul-winning in the past has been, or what the excuses of inactive church members may be, the fact remains that it is possible for us to improve our service along this line in the future. More than that, it is imperative that we as individuals become soul-winners if we are to meet the demands and win the approval of him who redeemed us and who commissioned us to continue the job of carrying his message of salvation to the lost until the last man, woman, boy, and girl in the world have had an opportunity to be saved.

And as the Bible contains the only authoritative word for Christians upon every other matter of duty, so it is quite full, clear, and emphatic on this most important of all phases of Christian service.

II. We Are Saved to Serve

1. Christ Called Us to Be Fishers of Men

Indicating the primacy of soul-winning, Christ announced to his first disciples, Peter, Andrew, James, and John, the Galilean fishermen, when he originally called them, that this would be their chief task. "Come ye after me, and I will make you fishers of men" (Matt. 4:19).

Back of the main task of the Christian, however, lies the primary task of the Saviour himself when he came to earth, for according to Luke 19:10, "The Son of man came to seek and to save that which was lost."

2. Christ Expects Us to Carry the Gospel to the Whole World

But it was not consistent with the heavenly plan for Christ to remain upon the earth indefinitely after he had completed his ministry, and before he ascended to be forever at the right hand of the Father he entrusted the carrying of the message of salvation to those who had already experienced the joy of the regenerated life.

Think for a moment what a tragedy it would have been to the lost millions on earth had the Lord reserved unto himself alone the task of carrying to all the world the story of his love! Someone has calculated that had the risen Saviour, instead of returning to heaven, begun a tour of India, for instance, on the day that he ascended, and had visited one village in that vast land each day, he would not yet have completed his visitation of that one country, and the rest of the world would yet be without any knowledge of him.

3. We Are Christ's Ambassadors to the Unsaved

For those of us who might hesitate to try and win others to Christ, it may help if we ponder the confidence and trust the Lord has imposed in us by making us his representatives, not to a court in another land but to all the world. The average man would consider

it the highest honor of life if he should be commissioned
by the President of the United States to become the
American ambassador at any foreign court, but in truth
we have been commissioned as ambassadors of Christ,
King of kings and Lords of lords! "We are ambassadors
therefore on behalf of Christ, as though God were
entreating by us: we beseech you on behalf of Christ,
be ye reconciled to God" (2 Cor. 5:20).

III. EVANGELISM IS OUR MAJOR TASK

1. *The Salvation of the Soul Is Fundamental*

Evangelism, including missions of course, is the major program of the churches and the supreme task of the
individual Christian.   This is true for many reasons,
but primarily because salvation is fundamental.   There
can be no spiritual growth in an individual until he
has first been born again and become a new creature in
Christ Jesus.   It was the great New England prophet
of a generation ago, Dr. Horace Bushnell, who said,
"The soul of reform is the reform of the soul."

Dr. George W. Truett, former president of the Baptist World Alliance, and of the Southern Baptist Convention, in his memorable presidential address before
the Atlanta session of the Alliance, in July, 1939, emphasized the primacy that belongs to evangelism in the
following words:

>   We must major on evangelism.   That is the first note
> in the marching orders of our risen Saviour and Lord.
> Evangelism is the missionary spirit in action.   It is the
> forerunner and builder of churches.   It is essential to
> all Christian expansion and must give its benign in-
> fluence to all sound teaching in the churches.   Dr. Duff
> well said: "The church that ceases to be evangelistic will
> soon cease to be evangelical."   In the New Testament
> everything goes out from the churches and draws back
> into the churches.   Whatever good may be done by
> methods and institutions apart from the churches, let
> us remember that Christ has put his honor in the

churches, and it needs to be urged with all emphasis that the hope of the people for a sound gospel, both for today and tomorrow, centers in the churches of the living God. "The church of the living God, the pillar and ground of the truth." And the first and supreme business of every church is to win souls to the salvation and service of Christ. This work is not secondary and incidental; it is primary and supreme. "As my Father hath sent me, even so send I you." "The Son of man is come to seek and to save that which was lost" (AV). If the seeking note for the salvation and training of souls be absent from a church, how much difference would there be between such church and an ethical club? All the estates of a church are to go afield, and stay afield, in this Christly work of winning souls to Christ.

2. *Churches Should Organize for Soul-Winning*

Dr. L. R. Scarborough, former president of the Southern Baptist Convention, long time president of the Southwestern Baptist Theological Seminary, and one of the great evangelists of this generation, once suggested that the churches must not only recognize evangelism as their major task, but must organize and consecrate their manpower to that end: "Our supreme challenge is massing, mobilizing, and utilizing our millions of men and money, millions of missionary-minded women and youth under the direction of the Holy Spirit for the winning of the lost."

3. *Baptists Could Improve Their Record*

For many years Southern Baptists have led the world in the total number of new members received into the churches by baptism, but what they are doing along that line is very small indeed compared to what they *ought* to do, and what they *could* do if each one of our approximately five million members would begin to measure up to his individual responsibility in this direction.

IV. Soul-Winning Is an Individual Responsibility

One of the greatest tragedies of all time is that the average Christian has allowed Satan to cheat him out of the joy of personal soul-winning. He defeats the Christian and makes him ashamed to talk to others about becoming Christians and deludes him into the belief that he is not responsible for the salvation of others.

Throughout the Bible there is emphasized the fact that we are saved to serve—to do whatever we can to win to Christ those immediately around us who are lost, and then by our prayers, gifts, and lives to assist in carrying the gospel to all the nations of the earth.

1. *Christ Expects Each One of Us to Win Others*

Note the emphasis which God's Word places upon individual responsibility in soul-winning, as represented in a few salient passages from both the Old and New Testaments:

"Even so let your light shine before men; that they may see your good works, and glorify your Father who is in heaven" (Matt. 5:16) is an exhortation from Christ himself. Note that the emphasis in this passage is on *your,* which is as individual as it is possible to make it. This means that each one of us who has been saved—man, woman, boy, or girl—is under orders from the Redeemer to do personal soul-winning. Not even the least of us is excused from that obligation.

2. *We Will be Held Accountable for Our Failures*

Not only are we under obligation personally to win the lost, but we will be held accountable to God for our failure to do so. Note the positiveness and directness of the Bible message upon this point.

> Son of man, I have made thee a watchman unto the house of Israel: therefore hear the word at my mouth, and give them warning from me. When I say unto the wicked, Thou shalt surely die; and thou givest him not

warning, nor speakest to warn the wicked from his
wicked way, to save his life; the same wicked man
shall die in his iniquity; but his blood will I require
at thy hand. Yet if thou warn the wicked, and he turn
not from his wickedness, nor from his wicked way, he
shall die in his iniquity; but thou hast delivered thy soul
(Ezek. 3:17-19).

In the light of this solemn, God-imposed responsibility, how is the average Christian going to fare when
he is called to account on this matter at the judgment
bar of God?

3. Our Responsibility Begins at Home

Our responsibility as individual soul-winners begins
in our own homes and extends out to the ends of the
earth. We recall the story of the violent demoniac
of Gadara who was healed by the Saviour and restored
to his right mind, and who wanted to show his gratitude
for what the Lord had done for him by accompanying
him on his ministry. There was little service he could
perform by merely joining the Lord's party, but there
was a great deal he could do by giving his personal
testimony to God's power among his own immediate
family, relatives, and friends; so it was perfectly natural that Christ "sent him away, saying, Return to thy
house, and declare how great things God hath done for
thee. And he went his way, publishing throughout the
whole city how great things Jesus had done for him"
(Luke 8:38-39).

And if this man out of whom Christ had just cast
many violent demons could become an effective witness, how can we who have been possessed of normal
faculties all our lives say that we cannot testify for our
Saviour? And note the simplicity of the message this
recently redeemed man was to convey to others. He
simply told them how great things Christ had done for
him. Every Christian who desires to win souls could
surely repeat the story of his own conversion, which

even the great apostle Paul did repeatedly in his testimonies for Christ.

It will probably help us realize our responsibility in the matter of winning others if we refresh our minds on God's interest in the unsaved, as set forth in this striking passage from the pen of Peter: "The Lord is not slack concerning his promise, as some count slackness; but is longsuffering to you-ward, not wishing that any should perish, but that all should come to repentance" (2 Peter 3:9).

Since God wills that none should perish, and has chosen us as the messengers to carry the knowledge of salvation to all men everywhere, surely he is looking to each one of us who has believed to help carry the gospel appeal to all unsaved men around the world.

All around each one of us there are literally thousands of lost persons, many of whom doubtless are looking to us to bring them the message of redemption. Can you imagine their disappointment when they realize that we do not think enough of our religion to try to bring others to embrace it? What if these unsaved ones should go into eternity lost, and should meet us with condemning eyes at God's judgment bar and inquire, "Oh, why did not you warn us of our impending doom?" Millions of lost souls on this day of final reckoning and probably throughout all eternity will be wailing to themselves, "No man careth for my soul" (Psalm 142:4)!

4. *Today's Opportunities May Be Gone Tomorrow*

Before we can begin to measure up to our responsibilities as personal soul-winners we must realize that the opportunities of today may be gone tomorrow, and frequently these opportunities will never return. Otherwise we may defer our purpose to speak to the unsaved about us until these persons are gone, and we shall have to report to our Lord, as did one of old, "And as thy servant was busy here and there, he was gone" (1 Kings 20:40).

V. Everyone Can Win Souls

1. *Holy Spirit Will Supply Worker's Needs*

It is recognized, of course, that the average Christian declares that he is totally incapable of winning others to Christ. But has that one ever made an effort in that direction to see whether he could succeed or not? Does he not understand that the Holy Spirit stands ready to accompany him as he goes forth on an evangelistic mission, and supply his every need?

2. *The Humblest Christian Can Win Lost if He Tries*

Many of the very humblest persons in the world have proved effective soul-winners. The great Dwight L. Moody, one of the most effective evangelists of all time, was only an uneducated shoe clerk when a tactful layman won him to Christ and enlisted him in Christian service.

Homer Rodeheaver, the great evangelistic singer, tells a remarkable story of how the most unpromising individual imaginable was used of God in winning nine other persons to Christ in one meetnig.

Several years ago when Mr. Rodeheaver and Mr. Sunday were on an evangelistic campaign in one of the midwestern states, there joined Mr. Rodeheaver's children's choir an afflicted boy named Joey. This lad had never been asked to do anything in the church before and was so pleased with the invitation to join the choir that he formed a fast friendship for Mr. Rodeheaver and would hang around at the close of the service each evening in order that he might be the last one to grasp the great singer's hand and bid him "goodnight." The boy's constant attention came near getting on Mr. Rodeheaver's nerves and he wanted at times to ask him to be less affectionate in his devotion. Recognizing the boy's handicap, however, he was patient with this constant attention.

On the next to the last night of the evangelistic campaign Mr. Rodeheaver noticed that a well-dressed man and woman of middle age, accompanied by five promising young people, evidently their children, came down to the front and gave Mr. Sunday their hands as an evidence of their acceptance of Jesus Christ as their Saviour. Then on the last night of the campaign a very old couple came down and made a similar profession.

After the benediction had been pronounced following the close of the final service a gentleman introduced himself to Mr. Rodeheaver as follows:

"Mr. Rodeheaver, I am Joey's father, and I want to thank you immensely for the courtesy you have shown my afflicted son. Never before has he been asked to participate in a religious service, but he has so greatly appreciated your interest in him and so happy is he in the opportunity for service which you have afforded him that he has constantly kept after all the family to come out to the meeting and hear you sing and Mr. Sunday preach.

"We have not been church people heretofore. Last night you probably noticed a man and his wife and five young people come down and give the evangelist their hands in confession of Jesus Christ as their Saviour. That group was composed of my wife and myself, and our five other children, and all of us became interested in the services and were finally led to Jesus Christ because of Joey's deep interest and his persistent invitations. Then tonight you may have noticed a very old couple come down and make a similar confession. They were Joey's grandparents; the grandfather was eighty-five years old and the grandmother eighty-one, both of whom had been professed infidels. Joey did not give them up, however, and kept inviting them to the services until they finally became interested and then eventually gave their hearts to God. So you see Joey has been instrumental in winning all of us, and I hope that knowledge will compensate you for your great courtesy to our afflicted son."

If this boy could be God's instrument in winning nine other persons to Jesus Christ, the remainder of us are left without excuse if we do not likewise go out and win souls.

3. *Boys and Girls Should Be Won in Early Life*

Every soul-winner should remember that it is far easier to win boys and girls to the Saviour than it is to win adult men and women. This does not mean that we should ignore men and women in our evangelistic efforts, but that, in the interest of achieving larger results, as well as in the hope of winning the entire life as well as the soul of the individual, we should be diligent in our efforts to win the boys and girls. Figures have been compiled to the effect that nine persons out of ten who become Christians do so before they are seventeen years old. This means that unless we win boys and girls to Christ before they reach that age the chances are nine to one they will go through life and into eternity without Christ.

VI. OUR FIELD IS THE WORLD

1. *Ours Is a Worldwide Commission*

Our whole duty in carrying out Christ's commission to make him known to the unsaved has not been done when we have merely spoken to the lost immediately about us and sought to bring them to an acceptance of Jesus Christ. That is merely the starting point in our evangelistic endeavor. Our full task has not been accomplished until we have done everything within our power in proclaiming Christ's power to save to the last lost individual in the whole world.

Christ said, "The field is the world" (Matt. 13:38). Not only is our field the world, but we have definite orders from the Saviour to take his gospel to all nations: "Go ye therefore, and make disciples of all

the nations" (Matt. 28:19).   This worldwide order of
Christ is emphasized further in these words:

> Go ye into all the world, and preach the gospel to the
> whole creation (Mark 16:15).
>
> And that repentance and remission of sins should be
> preached in his name unto all the nations, beginning
> from Jerusalem (Luke 24:47).
>
> And ye shall be my witnesses both in Jerusalem, and
> in all Judaea and Samaria, and unto the uttermost part
> of the earth (Acts 1:8).

2. *Over Billion People Do Not Yet Know Christ*

Recent figures indicate that after nineteen hundred
years there are considerably more than 1,500,000,000
adherents to heathen religions, in addition to the millions of unsaved persons in so-called Christian lands.

3. *Heathen Are Bringing Their Ideas to America*

One of the challenging factors in this dark picture is
the fact that the adherents of these non-Christian faiths
have been in the past, and are still today, far more
diligent in pushing the claims of their false religions
than are the average members of our Christian churches
in the promotion of the true faith.   Evidence of this fact
is found in the presence of 100 Buddhist temples in our
own United States.   In fact, the two largest heathen
temples in the world are located in the United States,
one of them at Los Angeles and the other in Chicago, it
is reported.

When Christ was on earth he said, "The fields . . . are
white already unto harvest" (John 4:35); and, "The
harvest indeed is plenteous, but the laborers are few"
(Matt. 9:37).   Those situations are even truer today.
God has literally opened the doors of evangelistic opportunity in practically every land under the sun in recent
years.   But in the light of all the need and opportunity,
Southern Baptists, with all their numbers and resources,
are supporting about 908 American missionaries in all
their thirty-four fields, and the average per capita gift

(1953) of Southern Baptists to the great cause of foreign missions is only about $1.11 per year! This is less than the cost of one ten-cent postage stamp per month. This means, of course, that many hundreds of thousands of church members do absolutely *nothing* for foreign missions, for many members give liberally. One member of the church to which the writer belongs gives $7,200 per year to foreign missions over and above her pledge to the regular church budget.

Can these hundreds of thousands of Southern Baptists who are doing little or nothing for the great cause of state, home, and foreign missions face our Lord in the last day and say sincerely that they really loved him when they were on the earth?

"We must work the works of him that sent me, while it is day: the night cometh, when no man can work" (John 9:4). If each one of us would heed this warning from the Master himself we would make opportunity now to redeem our failures of the past.

Some years ago there died in Texas a noble school-teacher who, in the course of her many years of service, had won more than 5,000 persons to the Saviour by her personal efforts, in addition to her contributions to missions from her meager salary through the years. How cordially she must have been greeted by the loving Saviour when she was called to her heavenly reward!

4. *Millions Lost in Southern Baptist Convention Territory*

In his effort to awaken members of our churches to a sense of their obligation to take the gospel message to the lost here in our own Convention territory, Dr. Roland Q. Leavell, former superintendent of evangelism for the Home Mission Board of the Southern Baptist Convention, wrote as follows in his gripping little tract, "Brightening Up Heaven":

Does your burning heart make you cry out warning to the lost, as did Jonah's when he cried out to Nineveh to repent? The thought of millions lost and unchurched people in our Convention territory should make any Christian weep like Jeremiah, when he lamented over Zion. Seeing that it requires 23 Southern Baptists an entire year to win one person to Christ, will you say with Isaiah, "Here am I, send me"? If our people could realize that of the 4,630 persons who die every hour, only 1,543 are even nominal Christians, surely they would utter the warning of Amos, "Prepare to meet thy God." Should not the 3,087 who died without Christ during the past hour cause every Christian heart to suffer a great heaviness and continual sorrow, like Paul's? Our Southern cities are seething with unsaved souls. Does your heart sob for these cities like the Saviour when he wept over Jerusalem? Only as the lamp of your heart burns can you light up heaven with the souls you have won to Christ.

More and more we need to join the poet who prayed this prayer:

> Lord, lay some soul upon my heart,
> And love that soul through me;
> And may I bravely do my part
> To win that soul to Thee.

VII. THE SOUL-WINNER NEEDS EQUIPMENT

To do effective soul-winning a Christian must possess among others, the following personal qualifications, according to God's Word:

1. Compassion for the lost — Psalm 126:5-6; Romans 10:1

2. Personal purity — Psalm 51:10-13; 66:18

3. Knowledge of the Bible — Ephesians 6:17

4. Wisdom — Proverbs 11:30

5. Faith — Mark 9:23; Isaiah 55:11

6. Patience — Ecclesiastes 11:1

7. Tact — Matthew 10:16

8. Diligence — Acts 20:31
9. Spiritual power — Acts 1:8

VIII. THE SOUL-WINNER GAINS RICH SATISFACTIONS

There is a brighter side to this question of the stewardship of evangelism, and that involves the satisfactions which the soul-winner reaps in this life, and the abundant rewards which God lays up for him in the world to come.

One of the satisfactions that come to the soul-winner, and probably the lowest one of them all, is that of a clear conscience: "Yet if thou warn the wicked, and he turn not from his wickedness, nor from his wicked way, he shall die in his iniquity; but thou hast delivered thy soul" (Ezek. 3:19).

Far more gratifying than the mere satisfaction of a clear conscience is the realization of the benefit one has conferred upon others in bringing them into a knowledge of salvation: "Let him know, that he who converteth a sinner from the error of his way shall save a soul from death, and shall cover a multitude of sins" (James 5:20).

Closely akin to the joy of saving souls from death is the realization of the fact that the soul-winner's influence upon others is generally uplifting: "How beautiful upon the mountains are the feet of him that bringeth good tidings, that publisheth peace, that bringeth good tidings of good, that publisheth salvation, that saith unto Zion, Thy God reigneth!" (Isa. 52:7).

Moreover, the soul-winner "gathereth fruit unto life eternal" (John 4:36). He will be proud to present to the Master the proof of his labors; for

"He that goeth forth and weepeth, bearing seed for sowing,

Shall doubtless come again with joy, bringing his sheaves with him" (Psalm 126:6).

Then those who have been faithful in soul-winning on earth will shine in the effulgence of God's glory forever in the world to come, we are assured in this passage: "And they that are wise shall shine as the brightness of the firmament; and they that turn many to righteousness as the stars for ever and ever" (Dan. 12:3).

This is the most definite guarantee of outstanding recognition in heaven that is given in the entire Bible. It would be wholly inconsistent with the spirit of true religion for us to want to stand out in heaven, for we should strive to win many souls in order that we may honor our Redeemer, who purchased our salvation by his death on the cross. But it is interesting to know that those of us who honor Christ in our lives will be greatly honored by the Father in the life to come.

When this life is ended, and we go out to be with God, we shall find that we are rewarded for every soul we have won to the Saviour by our personal effort, our public testimony, our consistent Christian conduct, our teaching and preaching, and our gifts to missions which result in sending the gospel to the unsaved beyond our own communities, in our states, in the nation at large, and around the world. And the more souls we win in this life the fuller and richer will our existence in heaven be throughout the long, long eternity. But to earn such rewards through the attainment of such a record we must be up and doing now, as we have been reminded by one who wrote:

Up and be doing! The time is brief,
And life is frail as the autumn leaf.
The day is bright and the sun is high;
Erelong it will fade from the glowing sky;
And the harvest is ripe and the fields are wide;
And thou, at thine ease, mayest not abide.
The reapers are few and far between,
And death is abroad with his sickle keen.
Go forth and labor! A crown awaits

The faithful servant at heaven's gates;
Work with thy might ere the day of grace
Is spent, ere the night steals on apace.
The Master has given his pledge divine,
"Who winneth souls like the stars shall shine."
                                    —ANONYMOUS

FOR FURTHER STUDY AND RESEARCH

1. Equip yourself for soul-winning by studying sugges-
   tions offered by such experienced soul-winners as P. E.
   Burroughs, L. R. Scarborough, and R. A. Torrey. Their
   books on this subject are listed in the bibliography in
   the back of this book.
2. Familiarize yourself with the fundamental Scripture
   passages on the plan of salvation, embodying such topics
   as "All have sinned" (Rom. 3:10–12, 23); "The wages
   of sin is death" (Rom. 6:23; Ezek. 3:18); "All must be
   born again" (John 3:1–16); "We are saved by grace,
   through faith, and not by works" (Eph. 2:8–9); "Youth
   is the best time to be saved" (Eccl. 12:1); "Christ will
   not turn away any sinner who comes to him" (John
   6:37; "Behold, now is the acceptable time" (2 Cor. 6:
   2); and "Thou shalt find him, when thou searchest
   after him with all thy heart and with all thy soul"
   (Deut. 4:29).

OUTLINE

I. WHY ARE WE NOT SOUL-WINNERS?
  1. Too Little Emphasis Given to Soul-Winning
  2. Average Church Member Unprepared for the Task
  3. Our Example Nullifies Our Influence
  4. We Have Little Compassion for the Lost

II. WE ARE SAVED TO SERVE
  1. Christ Called Us to Be Fishers of Men
  2. Christ Expects Us to Carry the Gospel to the Whole World
  3. We Are Christ's Ambassadors to the Unsaved

III. EVANGELISM IS OUR MAJOR TASK
  1. The Salvation of the Soul Is Fundamental
  2. Churches Should Organize for Soul-Winning
  3. Baptists Could Improve Their Record

IV. SOUL-WINNING IS AN INDIVIDUAL RESPONSIBILITY
  1. Christ Expects Each One of Us to Win Others
  2. We Will Be Held Accountable for Our Failures
  3. Our Responsibility Begins at Home
  4. Today's Opportunities May Be Gone Tomorrow

V. EVERYONE CAN WIN SOULS
  1. Holy Spirit Will Supply Worker's Needs
  2. The Humblest Christian Can Win Lost If He Tries
  3. Boys and Girls Should Be Won in Early Life

VI. OUR FIELD IS THE WORLD
  1. Ours Is a Worldwide Commission
  2. Over Billion People Do Not Yet Know Christ
  3. Heathen Are Bringing Their Ideas to America
  4. Lost in Southern Baptist Convention Territory— 47,872,117

VII. THE SOUL-WINNER NEEDS EQUIPMENT

VIII. THE SOUL-WINNER GAINS RICH SATISFACTIONS

CHAPTER VII

THE STEWARDSHIP OF PRAYER

I. WHY BE HUNGRY IN THE MIDST OF PLENTY?

Thousands of churches in the land, as well as the majority of the members of those churches, have failed to avail themselves of the spiritual power that might be theirs if they followed the example of the early Christians and tarried in the upper room until they, too, were endued with power from on high.

Could you imagine an intensely hungry man walking past a large table, heavily laden with all sorts of appetizing food, free for the taking, and not helping himself to such food as would satisfy his hunger? Such folly would mark him as mentally unsound. But we see hundreds of millions of professing Christians going through life with their souls greatly undernourished, and that in the midst of God's unlimited bounty from which we are free to choose just those foods that are needed to make us strong, happy, and useful.

1. *"Ye Have Not, Because Ye Ask Not"*

As was the case in the day of John the Baptist, so it is today, "A man can receive nothing, except it have been given him from heaven" (John 3:27). We could not live an hour without using the resources which a generous Heavenly Father places at our disposal without our asking, or frequently without our consciousness as to their origin. But these blessings which we enjoy without seeking are very small indeed compared to the larger benefits and satisfactions that would be ours if we only went to God and asked for them. As James reminded us in his epistle, "Ye have not, because ye ask not" (James 4:2).

2. *God Stands Ready to Supply Our Needs*

On the other hand we are assured by Paul that, "My God shall supply every need of yours according to his riches in glory in Christ Jesus" (Phil. 4:19). Are we not without excuse, then, when we continue merely to exist in the Christian life, lacking grace and strength with which to accomplish that growth in personal character and that usefulness in God's service that would be acceptable to him who made us, who provided our redemption through his only beloved Son, and who surrounds each one of us from day to day with all the uncounted blessings that are ours?

3. Churches Should Put New Emphasis on Prayer

Southern Baptists, with their more than nine million church members, their large number of church organizations, their capable pastors and other leaders, their orthodox doctrines, and the consecration of their enormous wealth, could easily become the most effective group of Christians the world has known since the apostolic era, if once they could catch a vision of their possibilities in prayer and then attain those possibilities by really engaging in that type of prayer which God's Word teaches us is acceptable to the Father.

Look for a moment at the midweek service in the average city church, by mistake called a prayer meeting. In literally thousands of the churches this midweek service consists chiefly of a sermonette by the pastor, or a brief address by a lay leader, or maybe a program by the Woman's Missionary Society, an Adult Sunday school class, or the Training Union. Now sermonettes, lay addresses, and programs by church organizations are thoroughly proper in their places; and frequently they are the means of accomplishing worthwhile results; but when they take the place of a genuine prayer service they result in the substitution of a smaller means of grace for an infinitely larger one.

And when the church as a whole ceases to major on prayer, it is only natural for church members, for the most part, to follow that example in their personal lives by giving less and less time to private prayer. The old-fashioned family altar is a thing of the past in the vast majority of Christian homes.

The testimony and service of the churches as organized units in the Master's service and the individual lives of the members of the churches will continue to be ineffectual until both the churches and their members come back to the point where they will give prayer the priority it merits. But when we do come to major in prayer, the spirituality of the lives of church members will be deepened, those members will become vitally concerned in the salvation of the lost at home and around the world, and they will begin to honor God with their means in a proportion that will be acceptable to him, thus bringing into the Lord's treasury all the resources that are needed to extend every phase of his kingdom to the ends of the earth.

II. We Stand in Need of Prayer

The average Christian does not pray more because he has not had a very definite feeling of his need of prayer. This makes it necessary that all of us make a new study of our need of fellowship with the Father in the light of his Word.

1. *Prayer Cleanses the Heart from Sin*

In the first place, we should pray more for the cleansing of our individual hearts from sin. Along with the psalmist, we should meditate upon our ways:

> Who can discern his errors?
> Clear thou me from hidden faults (Psalm 19:12).

> Have mercy upon me, O God, according to thy loving-kindness:
> According to the multitude of thy tender mercies blot out my transgressions.
> Wash me thoroughly from mine iniquity,
> And cleanse me from my sin. . . .
> Create in me a clean heart, O God;
> And renew a right spirit within me (Psalm 51:1-2, 10).

2. *Prayer Gives Strength for Daily Tasks*

But we need to pray not alone for personal cleansing from sin, but also that we may receive the grace and strength for performing the tasks God would have us do. It is an exceedingly easy matter for the average Christian, not fully instructed in God's Word, to overlook the fact that he is wholly insufficient in himself for living the acceptable life. More and more each of us needs to realize the deep significance of our Saviour's declaration: "I am the vine, ye are the branches: He that abideth in me, and I in him, the same beareth much fruit: for apart from me ye can do nothing" (John 15:5). Prayer is the service line through which Christ's power flows into our hearts.

Moreover, every Christian needs a new realization of the fact that all the power of Christ lies at the disposal of that believer who trusts him absolutely and abides fully in him. On this point we have not only the assurance of Paul, who followed Christ more completely and enjoyed his power more fully perhaps than any other Christian who ever lived, but also the unreserved declaration of the Lord himself. Paul's testimony was, "My God shall supply every need of yours according to his riches in glory in Christ Jesus" (Phil. 4:19), while the unqualified statement of Christ reads, "If ye abide in me, and my words abide in you, ask whatsoever ye will, and it shall be done unto you" (John 15:7).

What a world of encouragement is afforded every child of God in these notable passages, particularly in the emphatic words of them! In Paul's statement the emphasis is upon the word "every." This means there is absolutely no need of ours which our Lord will not supply, provided we are in the right relation to him and approach him in prayer as we ought. We need to make a distinction, however, between our *needs* and our *wants*. The average individual wants a great many things which he does not need—some of which would actually prove a detriment if he possessed them. That fact explains why God does not give us many of the things for which we pray. God answers every sincere prayer of his children, but he answers many of them by refusing to give us the things for which we ask, and substituting for those things which he denies us still better things that we need.

In the reassuring words from Christ the emphasis is on four points, two of them being conditions to acceptable prayer. The first of these is embodied in the phrase, "If ye abide in me," and the second, "and my words abide in you." Before we can claim Christ's great promise here, then, we must first be in full fellowship with him and must be doing his revealed will. If we meet these two fundamental conditions we are prepared to claim the possibilities implied in the remainder of the passage, Ye shall "ask whatsoever ye will, and it shall be done unto you." Note the unlimited possibilities in the two key words here: "whatsoever," a word to which there is no limit, and "shall," which is as positive as language can express.

There can be absolutely no power in the Christian's life aside from prayer, but all power is available to the Christian through acceptable prayer.

III. God Calls to Prayer

1. *The Call Is Sounded Throughout the Bible*

Not only did God make it possible for his children to have power through prayer, but he earnestly desired that they should avail themselves of this power from day to day. More than that, he gave repeated commands to Christians to ask for that power. So great is the goodness and generosity of the Heavenly Father that he gives us the exalted privilege of commanding him to confer that power upon us. Could the human mind conceive a greater privilege than that of commanding the God of all the universe? But that is exactly what God says in his Word upon this matter, as

witness these passages selected from among a large
number of others of similar import:

Call unto me, and I will answer thee, and will show
thee great things, and difficult, which thou knowest not
(Jer. 33:3).

If my people, who are called by my name, shall humble themselves, and pray, and seek my face, and turn
from their wicked ways; then will I hear from heaven,
and will forgive their sin, and will heal their land (2
(Chron. 7:14).

And it shall come to pass that, before they call, I will
answer; and while they are yet speaking, I will hear
(Isa. 65:24).

Concerning the work of my hands, command ye me
(Isa. 45:11).

But thou, when thou prayest, enter into thine inner
chamber, and having shut thy door, pray to thy Father
who is in secret, and thy Father who seeth in secret shall
recompense thee (Matt. 6:6).

2. *God Stands Ready to Answer All Sincere Prayer*

According to these promises God stands ready to
perform miracles in answer to sincere, earnest, believ-
ing prayer. He will forgive us our individual and social
sins, remove the punishments he has levied upon us
because of our disobedience, and remove the curses
from our land. So anxious is God to bless us that if
we come into the right attitude he will even answer
our petitions before we have had an opportunity to
utter them. So unlimited is the Father's love for us
that he even grants us the privilege of commanding
him concerning the work of his own hands. But for
our prayer life to be acceptable in his sight we must
supplement our public prayers with our secret devo-
tions, when none but God sees our attitudes and no
ears but his hear the earnest expression of our inner-
most thoughts.

In the light of all these wonderful revelations concerning God's command and promises concerning

prayer, how can we account for the spiritual poverty of the average Christian? Have we not allowed Satan to cheat us in the greatest swindle in all history?

Before we can claim God's promises in prayer, however, we must meet his conditions and pray in earnest. Three hundred years ago this truth was evident to Shakespeare, who made the king in *Hamlet* say,

> My words fly up, my thoughts remain below:
> Words without thoughts never to heaven go.

This idea has been elaborated upon by a modern poet who wrote:

> To *say* my prayers is not to pray
> Unless I *mean* the words I say;
> Unless I *think* to *whom* I speak,
> And with my heart His blessing seek.
> Then let me, when I come to pray,
> Not only heed the words I say,
> But let me seek with earnest care
> To have my thoughts go with my prayer.
> —ANONYMOUS

IV. THE LIST OF PRAYER OBJECTS IS ALMOST UNLIMITED

There are many Christians who say they do not pray because they do not know what to pray for. Here again the Bible comes to the assistance of all earnest seekers after truth by pointing out to them a number of things it is proper to seek in prayer. Only a few of these objects are listed here.

1. Forgiveness of sins. "And forgive us our sins" (Luke 11:4).
2. Personal cleansing.
   "Create in me a clean heart, O God;
   And renew a right spirit within me" (Psalm 51:10).
3. Victory over temptation. "Watch and pray, that ye enter not unto temptation" (Matt. 26:41).

4. Our physical needs. "Give us this day our daily bread" (Matt. 6:11).

5. Our enemies. "Love your enemies, and pray for them that persecute you" (Matt. 5:44).

6. All men. "I exhort therefore, first of all, that supplications, prayers, intercessions, thanksgivings, be made for all men; for kings and all that are in high place; that we may lead a tranquil and quiet life in all godliness and gravity" (1 Tim. 2:1-2).

7. Recovery from sickness. "Is any among you sick? let him call for the elders of the church; and let them pray over him, anointing him with oil in the name of the Lord: and the prayer of faith shall save him that is sick, and the Lord shall raise him up; and if he have committed sins, it shall be forgiven him" (James 5:14-15).

8. Wisdom in solving problems. "But if any of you lacketh wisdom, let him ask of God, who giveth to all liberally and upbraideth not; and it shall be given him" (James 1:5).

9. The coming of Christ's kingdom. "Thy kingdom come. Thy will be done, as in heaven so on earth" (Matt. 6:10).

10. Additional laborers in God's vineyard. "Pray ye therefore the Lord of the harvest, that he send forth laborers into his harvest" (Matt. 9:38).

11. One another. "Pray one for another" (James 5:16).

12. Our missionaries. "Brethren, pray for us" (1 Thess. 5:25).

In the consideration of things for which we are justified in praying, it is needful that we remember the character of God, that he is our Heavenly Father, who is far more concerned for us than our own parents ever were, who has all our best interests at heart, who is abundantly able to supply all our genuine needs; and, as Christ reminded us in his teachings, our Father is far wiser in providing us with good gifts than any earthly parent could possibly be.

V. There Are Many Hindrances to Prayer

Before we can pray acceptably—and only acceptable prayer brings results—it is needful that we understand the chief hindrances to prayer and remove them. Some of these hindrances are listed here:

1. *Iniquity in the Heart*

   "If I regard iniquity in my heart,
   The Lord will not hear" (Psalm 66:18).

2. *Unbelief*

   "But let him ask in faith, nothing doubting: for he that doubteth is like the surge of the sea driven by the wind and tossed. For let not that man think that he shall receive any thing of the Lord; a double-minded man, unstable in all his ways" (James 1:6-8).

3. *Selfishness*

   "Ye ask, and receive not, because ye ask amiss, that ye may spend it in your pleasures" (James 4:3).

4. *Pride*

   "God resisteth the proud, but giveth grace to the humble" (James 4:6).

5. *Unforgiving Spirit*

   "But if ye forgive not men their trespasses, neither will your Father forgive your trespasses" (Matt. 6:15).

6. *Neglect of God's Word*

   "He that turneth away his ear from hearing the law,

Even his prayer is an abomination" (Prov. 28:9).

7. *Disobedience*

"Beloved, if our heart condemn us not, we have boldness toward God; and whatsoever we ask we receive of him, because we keep his commandments and do the things that are pleasing in his sight" (1 John 3:21-22).

For our encouragement let it be emphasized that when any one of us is deeply in earnest about the matter of praying, God will come to his assistance and help remove from his heart every obstacle that stands in the way of acceptable communion with his Father.

VI. PREVAILING PRAYER HAS FOUR ELEMENTS

Christ's original disciples felt the need of instruction in how to pray, and in response to their request the Lord gave them what has come to be known as the Lord's Prayer, though a better title for it would doubtless be the Model Prayer.

In this connection it is well that all students remember that prayer consists of more than the mere recital of our needs to God. Judging from the prayers published in God's Word and instructions contained therein on prayer, acceptable prayer in the sight of God consists of the elements of adoration, thanksgiving, and intercession, as well as direct petitions for ourselves.

1. *Adoration*

Adoration in prayer consists of the direct worship of God, as represented in the introduction to the Lord's Prayer, "Our Father who art in heaven, Hallowed be thy name." In other words, adoration is telling God how we love and appreciate him and how much we desire to exalt his name.

2. *Thanksgiving*

Closely akin to adoration, and frequently illustrated in both the Old and New Testaments as an essential element in prayer, though not specifically mentioned in the Lord's Prayer, is thanksgiving. Just as the earthly parent is delighted at the appreciation of his child, our Heavenly Father is pleased when we show genuine gratitude for those blessings he has already bestowed upon us.

3. *Intercession*

Intercession involves pleading with God on behalf of others, such as asking him to restore the sick to health, comfort the sorrowing, provide for the needy, and bless the varied interests of his kingdom in the world. This aspect of prayer was emphasized by the Saviour in the passage, "Thy kingdom come, Thy will be done, as in heaven, so on earth."

4. *Petition*

Then in prayer for forgiveness of sin, for delivery from temptation, and for daily bread we have illustrations of personal petitions. The Heavenly Father is interested in having us come before him with all our personal needs, but for us to concentrate all our praying upon that aspect of prayer is to overlook those larger phases of true prayer—adoration of the Father, Christ, and the Holy Spirit; sincere gratitude for God's past blessings; and intercession in behalf of the many phases of God's work in the world and all those in the world for whom we should count it a privilege to pray. It is largely as we exercise ourselves in adoration, thanksgiving, and intercession that we really grow in spiritual strength through prayer. Those who concentrate their efforts in prayer to asking things solely for themselves will never become great Christians, because until one's vision is extended to include the whole world, and until he has developed a sense of genuine gratitude, his soul will continue dwarfed indeed.

VII. Genuine Praying Is Hard Work

One of the main reasons so few Christians have grown great in prayer is that praying is hard work. It entails a mental alertness, concentration, purpose, and earnestness of desire that are entirely foreign to the lazy soul. It is very easy therefore, as has already been intimated, for Satan to slip into our hearts and divert us from our main purpose in prayer. Satan has no fear of God's people when they assemble in conventions, conferences, assemblies, rallies, and other types of general public meetings, as sincere as the purposes rallies, and other types of general public meetings, of all such gatherings may be, if they leave prayer out of the meeting; but when God's people in large numbers begin to pray genuinely, singly or in meetings, then the evil one becomes excited, for he knows that God works through praying people. When God is able to work through his children, then the power of darkness is doomed to defeat.

VIII. All Things Are Possible in Prayer

While much has already been intimated of the possibilities of prayer, there is need of further emphasis upon this very vital aspect of communion with God.

All successful prayer is dependent upon wholehearted earnestness and concentration, as God himself pointed out through one of his prophets of the long ago: "And ye shall call upon me, and ye shall go and pray unto me, and I will hearken unto you. And ye shall seek me, and find me, when ye shall search for me with all your hearts" (Jer. 29:12-13).

Some of the additional passages suggesting the large possibilities that lie open to every one of us in prayer, if we are willing to pay God's price for power, follow:

All things are possible to him that believeth (Mark 9:23).

If ye have faith as a grain of mustard seed, ye shall say unto this mountain, Remove hence to yonder place;

and it shall remove; and nothing shall be impossible unto you (Matt. 17:20).

He that believeth on me, the works that I do shall he do also; and greater works than these shall he do; because I go unto the Father. And whatsoever ye shall ask in my name, that will I do, that the Father may be glorified in the Son. If ye shall ask anything in my name, that will I do (John 14:12-14).

Ask, and it shall be given you; seek, and ye shall find; knock, and it shall be opened unto you: for every one that asketh receiveth; and he that seeketh findeth; and to him that knocketh it shall be opened (Matt. 7:7-8).

It is encouraging to note that God does not put all the burden of fellowship with him upon us. He actually comes to our own hearts' doors and seeks admission, as revealed in this gracious passage: "Behold, I stand at the door and knock: if any man hear my voice and open the door, I will come in to him, and will sup with him, and he with me" (Rev. 3:20).

But the full possibilities of prayer have not been explored until we have comprehended, in part at least, what, in this writer's estimation, is probably the most marvelous verse in the whole Bible: "Now unto him that is able to do exceeding abundantly above all that we ask or think, according to the power that worketh in us" (Eph. 3:20). This verse tells us that so unlimited is the power of God, and so generous is his disposition toward us, his children, that he is able to do far more for us than we are able to ask, or even think.

Finally, we read that when our Lord was upon the earth he frequently spent whole nights in prayer, particularly when he was faced with tremendous responsibilities the next day. On other occasions, Christ slept a little while and then "a great while before day" went out alone to commune with the Father. If our Lord, who was very God as well as very man, needed this communion with heaven in order to accomplish his work fully, how much more do we need to talk with

God and seek his strength for the tasks that await us!

When we, as Christians, actually come to imitate our Master in prayer, his kingdom will come speedily.

FOR FURTHER STUDY AND RESEARCH

1. Few projects of Bible study could prove more interesting and profitable than a careful searching of the Scriptures for everything said on prayer. A good concordance and parallel reference Bible will be of invaluable assistance.
2. Follow this up with a devotional reading of the great prayers of the Bible.
3. Then make a special study of God's promises to hear and answer prayer, as contained in both the Old and New Testaments.
4. Reread the Four Gospels and make a special memorandum on the prayer life of Jesus.
5. Select a half-dozen of the most outstanding promises of God to hear and answer prayer, and put God to the test on them.
6. Try a half hour of Bible study and prayer each morning before you leave your room, eat breakfast, glance at your daily paper, or turn on the radio.
7. Establish a family altar in your home.
8. Organize a prayer league in your church.

OUTLINE

I. WHY BE HUNGRY IN THE MIDST OF PLENTY?
1. "Ye Have Not, Because Ye Ask Not"
2. God Stands Ready to Supply Our Needs
3. Churches Should Put New Emphasis on Prayer
II. WE STAND IN NEED OF PRAYER
1. Prayer Cleanses the Heart from Sin
2. Prayer Gives Strength for Daily Tasks
III. GOD CALLS TO PRAYER
1. The Call Is Sounded Throughout the Bible
2. God Stands Ready to Answer All Sincere Prayer
IV. THE LIST OF PRAYER OBJECTS IS ALMOST UNLIMITED

V. THERE ARE MANY HINDRANCES TO PRAYER
   1. Iniquity in the Heart
   2. Unbelief
   3. Selfishness
   4. Pride
   5. Unforgiving Spirit
   6. Neglect of God's Word
   7. Disobedience

VI. PREVAILING PRAYER HAS FOUR ELEMENTS
   1. Adoration
   2. Thanksgiving
   3. Intercession
   4. Petition

VII. GENUINE PRAYING IS HARD WORK

VIII. ALL THINGS ARE POSSIBLE IN PRAYER

CHAPTER VIII

HAPPINESS HERE AND HEREAFTER

Did you ever stop to ponder how you will spend your time in the long eternity in the Heavenly Father's house, provided you are so fortunate as to be admitted there? Or did you ever give any thought to just how happy you will be in heaven?

God's Word may not be as full and explicit on these points as some of us might wish, but it does imply very definitely that there will be degrees of happiness in heaven, each one's measure of satisfaction being determined by the fulness and loyalty of his service to the Master here on earth. God is no respecter of persons in this life, and he will play no favorites in the hereafter. Many members of our churches who have been most prominent economically and socially in this world may be very inconspicuous in heaven, because they did so little service for the Master in proportion to their ability. On the other hand, other persons of very humble social station and of very slender economic resources here below, who used their small talents and means for the glory of God, will find an abundant reward awaiting them in heaven because they "did what they could."

Someone has told the imaginative story of a very prominent society matron who, following her death, knocked at the door of heaven and asked to be shown to the mansion which the Saviour had prepared for her. The record-keeper is reputed to have examined his books and then advised her: "I am very sorry to report that we have no mansion reserved for you. I find, however, that there is a small bungalow over on the back side of heaven that has been set aside for you. I will gladly escort you to it."

As the two were walking along the golden streets, they passed a beautiful mansion and the matron pleaded, "Why cannot I have that beautiful mansion there?"

"Oh, that mansion belongs to a faithful servant, who utilized every opportunity he had on earth to serve his Master," the escort replied.

The Christian who has expended all his means on himself and his family, giving little to God and contributing even that small amount grudgingly, will discover very little reward, if any, laid up for him in heaven. We shall find nothing to our credit there, other than eternal life, save those dividends and rewards which will have accumulated as a result of our service for the Lord here on the earth.

On the other hand, if we have been faithful in life in the use of all the resources which God has entrusted to us, we shall find abundant rewards awaiting us at the hands of the Heavenly Father, whether our names have ever appeared in print here or not.

However, one does not have to wait until he enters his eternal abode to begin enjoying the satisfactions of the stewardship life, for the faithful steward is exceedingly happy here on earth.

What are some of the rewards of faithful stewardship?

I. THE FAITHFUL STEWARD HAS A GOOD CONSCIENCE

One reason so few Christians are genuinely happy is that their consciences hurt them, not always because they have committed some disgraceful, immoral act, but because they have failed to live up to the high standards of stewardship which they know God has set for them. But the Christian who sets aside out of his income, before he spends any of it on himself, an adequate portion for God's cause; who utilizes his time, talents, influence, and all his other resources for the glory of God, is genuinely happy, because his conscience is clear and he enjoys in his mind and heart the approval of the Lord.

Paul, who lived the most strenuous Christian life of all followers of Christ through all the ages, gave himself and all his powers more unreservedly to the service of the Master, following his conversion, than any other has done. It is no wonder then that the great apostle was able to declare, "Brethren, I have lived before God in all good conscience until this day" (Acts 23:1). The maintenance of this attitude was a definite policy with this apostle, for he sought to keep his conscience clear toward his fellow men, as well as toward God, as set forth in his words, "Herein I also exercise myself to have a conscience void of offence toward God and men always" (Acts 24:16).

When the mother of James and John, shortly before Christ's crucifixion went to the Saviour and asked that her sons might sit, one on the right hand and the other on the left hand of the Lord in heaven, Jesus replied that these positions of great honor were reserved by the Father, to be filled as he had planned. This writer has always believed that the position of highest honor among God's redeemed children in the world to come would undoubtedly belong to Paul, for surely none other so far has served his Redeemer with so great efficiency and fidelity.

It is not permitted to any of us to match the talents and services of Paul, of course, but if each one of us should measure up to our abilities and opportunities with even a small measure of the industry and loyalty that characterized the great Apostle to the Gentiles, we would insure ourselves a very happy sojourn here on earth and an abundant reward in heaven. God rewards according to ability and faithfulness, we will remember, "And to whomsoever much is given, of him shall much be required: and to whom they commit much, of him will they ask the more" (Luke 12:48).

II. THE LORD APPROVES THE FAITHFUL STEWARD

While the satisfaction of a good conscience is a tremendous incentive to faithful stewardship, an even higher consideration is the approval of God, of which the faithful steward is always assured. From an abundant volume of teaching in the Bible we are convinced that God never allows the smallest service to him or needy humanity, in his name, to go unrewarded. We quote only a few passages to suggest the approval of the Lord's faithful stewards, particularly in the matter of putting the claims of God first, honoring him with our means, and winning the lost to the Saviour:

Honor Jehovah with thy substance,
And with the first-fruits of all thine increase:
So shall thy barns be filled with plenty,
And thy vats shall overflow with new wine
(Prov. 3:9-10).

The liberal soul shall be made fat;
And he that watereth shall be watered also himself
(Prov. 11:25).

Wheresoever the gospel shall be preached throughout the whole world, that also which this woman hath done shall be spoken of for a memorial of her (Mark 14:9).

Give, and it shall be given unto you; good measure, pressed down, shaken together, running over, shall they give into your bosom. For with what measure ye mete it shall be measured to you again (Luke 6:38).

He that soweth sparingly shall reap also sparingly; and he that soweth bountifully shall reap also bountifully (2 Cor. 9:6).

Verifications of these promises from God's Word in the actual experiences of his devoted servants are evident in practically every congregation that includes in its membership any faithful stewards.

Several interesting illustrations have fallen under the observation of this writer. A teen-age lad who was working hard to help support his family wanted very much to get a new winter suit of clothes as the other members of his Sunday school class had, but he had denied himself that privilege because of his loyalty to his family. Finally, the mother decided the time had come when the family should deny itself a bit in order that this son might have a new suit. Accordingly, she arranged to let him keep a whole week's wages with which to purchase the suit.

When the son went to church Sunday morning, however, he heard an eloquent appeal for foreign missions and decided to deny himself the suit in order that he might give the whole week's wages to missions. The next day when he reported for work he was informed by his boss that his monthly wages had been increased by the amount he had given to missions, and so he was able both to make his sacrificial gift to missions and to procure his needed suit of clothes.

The late J. F. Jarman, active Christian layman of Nashville, Tennessee, was for a number of years vice-president and sales manager of a large shoe factory in that city. He was a faithful steward and longed to see the day when he might own a factory himself and operate the business as he believed God would have him do. On several occasions, as the passing years would draw to a close, Mr. Jarman would approach the president of the concern and ask the privilege of resigning; but so valuable were his services to the business that the president would persuade him to stay with the concern by increasing both his salary and his commission.

Finally, as Mr. Jarman approached the age of sixty, he decided that if he was ever to establish a business of his own and operate it on a definitely Christian basis, he would have to do so soon; so he resolved to settle the matter once for all.

Taking a day off from work in the interim between Christmas and New Year's, this Christian businessman drove out to a little town not far from Nashville, engaged a room at a hotel, and instructed the clerk that he must not be disturbed by anyone or any type of call or interruption at any hour that day.

Entering the room, Mr. Jarman got down on his knees before his open Bible, read a number of passages from the book, and then prayed earnestly that God would reveal to him unmistakably what his will for him was in the matter of going into business for himself. As the day wore on this good man received what he interpreted as a definite answer from God that he should relinquish all connections with the older firm, enter business for himself, and take God into his partnership in the conduct of his factory and in the disposition of the profits of the concern.

Having received his answer from the Lord, Mr. Jarman lost no time in acting upon it by resigning promptly all previous connections with the older shoe company and launching a business of his own. After securing a site and building his factory in Nashville, he got his business under way about the middle of August and made a net profit in excess of $20,000 by the end of the year. Businessmen recognize this record as a very unusual one.

The young business was fairly well established by the time the financial debacle of 1929 occurred, and throughout the depression that followed the sales of this company continued to mount until now the company is recognized as one of the major shoe companies of America.

Mr. Jarman had been a faithful tither for many years prior to going into business for himself. He believed his employees were entitled to adequate wages, the very best of working conditions, expert medical and dental service, and an opportunity to become shareholders in the company; so he promptly put these various provisions into operation.

Before he died in 1938 he had set up a foundation for the promotion of special Christian enterprises in which he was vitally interested, and so liberally had God prospered him in business he had been able to place more than a million dollars into that foundation, in addition to making adequate provision for the members of his family. The writer has known scores of

Christian businessmen who were faithful stewards of God, and he has never known one whom God did not prosper in his own spiritual life and in his business or profession also.

III. WE SHARE IN EXTENDING GOD'S KINGDOM

Another great satisfaction of the faithful steward is that which comes from the knowledge that he has a definite share in extending God's kingdom in the world. Over and over again in the Bible we are assured that the Lord never allows one of his servants to go unrewarded for any deed of service, no matter how humble that service may be. Even one kind word spoken to an unsaved soul or a discouraged person, or one cup of cold water given to a thirsty individual in the name of the Saviour is always recognized and rewarded by the kind Heavenly Father.

For our encouragement let's examine a few direct quotations from our infallible guide, the Word of God:

Cast thy bread upon the waters; for thou shalt find it after many days (Eccl. 11:1).

Blessed are ye that sow beside all waters (Isa. 32:20).

He that goeth forth and weepeth, bearing seed for sowing,

Shall doubtless come again with joy, bringing his sheaves with him (Psalm 126:6).

How beautiful upon the mountains are the feet of him that bringeth good tidings, that publisheth peace, that bringeth good tidings of good, that publisheth salvation, that saith unto Zion, Thy God reigneth! (Isa. 52:7).

There is no question that every individual who is faithful in the exercise of his stewardship, not alone of means but of time, talents, influence, prayer, and all the other resources at the Christian's command, will have a very definite share in extending God's kingdom in the world and will begin to reap dividends upon those investments even in this world.

Bible students will recall the story of David's division of the spoils, following his successful raid upon the Amalekites, when the future king of Israel recovered not only his two wives who had been taken from him, but a large amount of spoils of varied character as well. David had left a number of his weaker men at the camp, while he and his able-bodied followers made the raid that resulted in the capture and slaughter of the enemy. Some of those who went into battle opposed any division of the spoils with those who guarded the baggage at the camp, but David showed his wisdom and humanity by ordering: "For as his share is that goeth down to the battle, so shall his share be that tarrieth by the baggage: they shall share alike" (1 Sam. 30:24).

This same principle is put into operation in his kingdom by the all-wise, just, and righteous Heavenly Father. He assures the faithful men and women, who invest their prayers, gifts, and other resources in extending the kingdom, that they shall share equally with the missionaries, evangelists, and other workers who minister to needy humanity in the name of the Saviour.

A Baptist merchant in North Carolina paid the salary of a Baptist missionary in China for many years. The missionary reported regularly concerning every phase of his work to this good layman who was supporting him. When the merchant wanted to acquaint others with the progress of this particular mission station in China he would always refer to the work there as "our" work. When he referred to the missionary he would characterize him as "my" missionary. Nor did this good layman exaggerate the situation. The work in China was actually his, in part, because his gifts made it possible, and this missionary was a partner of this merchant, who could not himself go and take the gospel message, just as he was also an ambassador of Jesus Christ. And when time ends and all the records of our work on earth are balanced on the books of heaven, this loyal merchant will find that he has had a share in the salvation of every soul whom the missionary won to Christ on the foreign field, and in every other good influence this man of God set in motion in the service of the Master.

All of us can have a definite and liberal share in promoting Christ's kingdom throughout the world if we will only become faithful stewards of God while we live.

Sometimes the Lord may have a different plan by which we should exercise our stewardship than that which we had preferred for ourselves; but all of us will recognize that his plan is far superior to ours and should be followed at all costs.

Many years ago a brilliant young Englishman had dedicated himself to God and prepared himself for missionary service on the foreign fields. But when time came for his physical examination, the mission board's physician found that the young man's constitution could not stand the strain of the climate in equatorial Africa, where the candidate had hoped to invest his life. The mission board sustained the findings of the physician and refused to appoint the applicant to service.

The young man's disappointment almost broke his heart at first, but he had long ago learned to lay all his problems before the Lord. When he took this biggest matter of his life to the throne of grace, the Heavenly Father revealed to him that he had it within his power to become a great physician in London, and that by giving his income to the mission board he could make possible the sending of numerous missionaries to Africa instead of going out himself. The young man accepted the Lord's home assignment and succeeded in his medical profession in a marvelous manner; and many years ago this London physician had sent out sixty missionaries from his liberal professional income and thus multiplied his mission ministry sixty-fold by remaining at home.

But the individual of modest means is also assured of having a share in extending God's kingdom when he comes to practice true stewardship. Dr. E. Y. Mullins once said: "The poor Scotch woman who, by hard labor and sacrifice, saved $60 and gave it to David Livingstone, the missionary and explorer, to provide for him an African body servant, was potentially a Livingstone. And when the body servant thus obtained saved Livingstone's life from the attack of a lion, she had given Livingstone for the remainder of his days."

IV. OUR ETERNAL DIVIDENDS ARE IN THE BANK OF HEAVEN

Not only does the faithful steward of all the resources which God has given him enjoy a good conscience, a sense of God's approval here on earth, and a share in extending Christ's kingdom out to the ends of the earth, but also he lays up for himself eternal dividends in the bank of heaven upon which he may draw just as heavily as he likes every day throughout the endless eternity.

It was in the hope of enabling all his children to enjoy an abundant entrance into heaven and the largest satisfactions there that the Master admonished us in his earthly ministry upon this very point:

> Lay not up for yourselves treasures upon the earth, where moth and rust consume, and where thieves break through and steal: but lay up for yourselves treasures in heaven, where neither moth nor rust doth consume, and where thieves do not break through nor steal (Matt. 6:19-20).

Thousands upon thousands of Americans had regarded themselves rich in this world's goods during the prosperous decade from 1920 to 1930, but when the bottom fell out of the speculative markets in the fall of 1929, many of these persons found their fortunes swept away before they could find any means of salvaging even a small portion of them, so fictitious were the values upon which they had been depending.

Futures in commodities, speculative stocks and bonds in industrial enterprises of many characters, and even in banks were suddenly found to be almost worthless. Even real estate which had been bought at highly speculative prices proved to be worth far less than the purchaser had contracted to pay. Droughts, famines, wars, and other calamities can sweep away even legitimate life savings on very short notice, but those investments which we have made in heaven, through the contributions of our means and our service in the kingdom of God, cannot be touched by the economic reverses here on earth. Our investments in stewardship are deposited by our Lord for us in the Eternal Bank of Heaven. There is no force in all the universe that can rob us of them, nor can any evil force interrupt the constant flow of the generous dividends God pays. If we have been faithful in our stewardship, we may confidently expect that we shall be very rich in the world to come.

The beloved Paul supplemented our Master's admonition on eternal investments with a very sharp warning against covetousness:

Charge them that are rich in this present world, that they be not highminded, nor have their hope set on the uncertainty of riches, but on God, who giveth us richly all things to enjoy; that they do good, that they be rich in good works, that they be ready to distribute, willing to communicate; laying up in store for themselves a good foundation against the time to come, that they may lay hold on the life which is life indeed (1 Tim. 6:17-19).

Selfishness and covetousness are not limited to the rich, it must be remembered. The poor man who refuses to honor God with what he has may be just as great a sinner in the eyes of God as is the rich man who refuses to give liberally. God is more interested in motives and spirit than he is in the size of one's gift.

V. GOD SHALL COMMEND US ON THE LAST DAY

The measure of our satisfaction throughout all eternity will be determined by the reception which Christ accords us when we face him at the judgment bar on the last day. The Lord reads all the intents of our minds and hearts. No camouflage, pretense, or boasting can pass the eye of God undetected. If after Christ has read and approved our record on earth, he welcomes us to his eternal abode with, "Well done, good and faithful servant: . . . enter thou into the joy of thy Lord," our joy will be supreme every day of the vast eternity. But if we have merely trusted Christ for salvation here on earth, and have done no service afterward in expression of our love and appreciation of all he did for us, we will be permitted to remain in heaven, but we shall find no reward waiting us. Our souls will be saved but our lives will have been lost.

Faithfulness is the basis of the heavenly commendation: And he that received the five talents came and brought other five talents, saying, Lord, thou deliveredst unto me five talents: lo, I have gained other five talents. His lord said unto him, Well done, good and faithful servant: thou hast been faithful over a few things, I will set thee over many things (Matt. 25:20-21).

One of the encouraging aspects of this study is afforded in the fact that the Lord will reward us for many humble services we have unconsciously performed for him, as set forth in this interesting statement from Christ himself.

But when the Son of man shall come in his glory, and all the angels with him, then shall he sit on the throne of his glory: and before him shall be gathered all the nations: and he shall separate them one from another, as the shepherd separateth the sheep from the goats; and he shall set the sheep on his right hand, but the goats on the left. Then shall the King say unto them on his right hand, Come, ye blessed of my Father, inherit the kingdom prepared for you from the foundation of the world: for I was hungry, and ye gave me to eat; I was thirsty, and ye gave me drink; I was a stranger, and ye took me in; naked, and ye clothed me; I was sick, and ye visited me; I was in prison, and ye came unto me. Then shall the righteous answer him, saying, Lord, when saw we thee hungry, and fed thee? or athirst, and gave thee drink? And when saw we thee a stranger, and took thee in? or naked, and clothed thee? And when saw we thee sick, or in prison, and came unto thee? And the King shall answer and say unto them, Verily I say unto you, Inasmuch as ye did it unto one of these my brethren, even these least, ye did it unto me. Then shall he say also unto them on the left hand, Depart from me, ye cursed, into the eternal fire which is prepared for the devil and his angels: for I was hungry, and ye did not give me to eat; I was thirsty, and ye gave me no drink; I was a stranger, and ye took me not in; naked, and ye clothed me not; sick, and in prison, and ye visited me not. Then shall they also answer, saying, Lord, when saw we thee hungry, or athirst, or a stranger, or naked, or sick, or in prison, and did not minister unto thee? Then shall he answer them, saying, Verily I say unto you, Inasmuch as ye did it not unto one of these least, ye did it not unto me. And these shall go away into eternal punishment: but the righteous into eternal life (Matt. 25:31-46).

But it is not necessary that we wait until we get to heaven to begin reaping the satisfactions and rewards from our wholehearted loyalty to Jesus Christ, a fact that is likewise made clear by a direct statement of the Lord himself:

"Jesus said, Verily I say unto you, There is no man that hath left house, or brethren, or sisters, or mother, or father, or children, or lands, for my sake, and for the gospel's sake, but he shall receive a hundredfold now in this time, houses, and brethren, and sisters, and mothers, and children, and lands, with persecutions; and in the world to come eternal life" (Mark 10: 29-30).

The commendation and reward for faithful service have already been provided and laid aside in heaven awaiting the arrival of the steward in the presence of his Lord, according to the inspired Paul, who wrote: "I have fought the good fight, I have finished the course, I have kept the faith: henceforth there is laid up for me the crown of righteousness, which the Lord, the righteous judge, shall give to me at that day; and not to me only, but also to all them that have loved his appearing" (2 Tim. 4:7-8).

With the exception of his early persecution of the church, in which he engaged with a clear conscience, Paul probably had fewer things on his record to blush for, when he was summoned into the presence of the Saviour, than any other one who has ever lived. And so far as the record is available to us, it would appear that he had larger rewards laid up for him in heaven than any other; for surely no other disciple of whom we know ever gave himself so wholeheartedly and unreservedly to the service of Christ. Few suffered greater hardships than he did, and almost singlehanded, though he was sustained in part by some of the churches and a few helpers, he carried the gospel to almost the whole known world, and that in a day when the methods of travel and communication were not a tenth so numerous, convenient, and efficient as they are today.

What if the Christians of today, even we Southern Baptists, could catch Paul's spirit for this generation? We could carry the gospel in its transforming power to the rest of the world within our own lifetime. Sin, with all its many attendant evils, could be largely eradicated from the world; and that glorious day when "the earth shall be filled with the knowledge of the glory of Jehovah, as the waters cover the sea" (Hab. 2:14) could be ushered in.

GOD'S BEST

God has his best things for the few
    Who dare to stand the test;
He has his second best for those
    Who will not have His best.

It is not always open ill
  That risks the promised rest;
The better often is the foe
  That keeps us from the best.

And others make the highest choice,
  But, when by trials pressed,
They shrink, they yield, they shun the Cross
  And so they lose the best.

Give me, O Lord, thy highest choice—
  Let others take the rest.
Their good things have no charm for me:
  I want thy very best.

I want, in this short life of mine,
  As much as can be pressed
Of service true for God and man;
  Make me to be thy best.

                                    —A. B. SIMPSON

FOR FURTHER STUDY AND RESEARCH

1. What will be the difference in the eternal status of the Christian who was a faithful steward of all the resources God entrusted to him and that of the one who merely trusted Christ for salvation but never did anything for the Saviour in return?

2. Summarize in a brief paper the general teachings of the Bible on rewards.

3. List the chief satisfactions which the faithful Christian will reap in this life.

4. Select the best Christian steward you know in your community and ask him to relate to you the compensations of an active Christian life.

OUTLINE

  I. THE FAITHFUL STEWARD HAS A GOOD CONSCIENCE
 II. THE LORD APPROVES THE FAITHFUL STEWARD
III. WE SHARE IN EXTENDING GOD'S KINGDOM
 IV. OUR ETERNAL DIVIDENDS ARE IN THE BANK OF HEAVEN
  V. GOD SHALL COMMEND US ON THE LAST DAY

QUESTIONS FOR REVIEW AND EXAMINATION

For instructions concerning the examination and the requesting of awards see Requirements for Credit in Class or Home Study, page vii.

CHAPTER I

1. Why did God make each individual different from every other person?
2. Give three reasons why all of us are God's and not our own.
3. If God has a plan for every life, what should be our duty in regard to his plan for our lives?
4. What is the meaning of the word "steward"?
5. What is the chief task of Christian stewards?
6. Cite three Scripture passages indicating that Christians are partners of God.

CHAPTER II

7. Summarize briefly the emphasis Christ placed upon the stewardship of possessions in his earthly ministry.
8. Cite two Scripture passages indicating that giving is essential to worship.
9. Show from scriptural authority that everything we have comes from God.
10. What is the lowest standard of giving suggested anywhere in the Bible?
11. What should be the attitude of the Christian toward tithing his income?
12. Sketch briefly the New Testament program for giving.
13. Cite three Bible promises of rewards to liberal givers.

CHAPTER III

14. Show wherein time is the most precious thing in the world.
15. Show wherein God has shown no favoritism in his distribution of time.
16. Cite three Scripture passages which show that life is short and uncertain at best.

17. Indicate some of the common ways in which most Christians waste much time.

18. On the basis of this chapter, make out a proper budget of your time for a week.

19. Show wherein idleness and laziness are condemned by God's Word.

20. How much of a layman's time should be set aside for the worship and service of God?

CHAPTER IV

21. Show wherein God expects a man of few talents, as well as the one of many, to use them in his service.

22. Indicate wherein God's program calls for service of every saved individual.

23. Suggest how it is incumbent upon every Christian to discover and use his talents.

24. Show how God will demand an accounting of how we have used our talents.

25. Indicate some of the special opportunities open to adults through the Sunday school.

26. Indicate the folly of passing up small opportunities while waiting for larger ones.

27. Show how the Lord never overlooks the smallest service performed in his name.

CHAPTER V

28. What Bible passages would you cite to prove that every person has some influence?

29. Cite at least two Bible passages that indicate the Christian's conduct should be much higher than the non-Christian's.

30. Why should a Christian consider his influence upon others in determining his conduct?

31. What aid does God provide the Christian in setting a good example?

32. Show wherein adults should strive to set worthy examples for young people and children.

33. What considerations prompt the Christian to honor God in his method of living?

34. Show wherein it is possible for one's soul to be saved while his works are destroyed.

CHAPTER VI

35. Why does the average church member not engage in personal soul-winning?
36. Indicate why Christ expects each Christian to win others.
37. Suggest why churches should concentrate upon evangelism and missions as their major task.
38. Suggest how every Christian can become a soul-winner if he tries.
39. Indicate briefly the world situation which demands that each one of us win souls.
40. What are the chief equipments for the soul-winner?
41. Suggest some of the soul-winner's satisfactions, both in this life and in the life to come.

CHAPTER VII

42. From your own experience and knowledge of human nature, suggest why Christians need to pray.
43. From your general knowledge of the Bible, suggest the numerous orders it contains to Christians to call upon God.
44. Make a list of at least a half-dozen things for which Christians should pray.
45. Indicate a half-dozen hindrances to effectual prayer set forth in God's Word.
46. From a study of what we know as the Lord's Prayer, show that genuine prayer consists of more than asking God for things we desire for ourselves.
47. Indicate how effective praying is hard work.
48. Cite at least five Bible passages which suggest the large possibilities which lie in true prayer.

CHAPTER VIII

49. How do you suppose we shall spend our time in heaven?
50. Why will some have more joy than others in heaven?
51. Locate at least three Scripture passages dealing with rewards in heaven.
52. Show wherein the faithful Christian steward does not

have to wait until he gets to heaven to begin reaping his rewards.

53. Name at least three satisfactions the true steward enjoys in this life.

54. Show how those at home who support missions abroad will have a share in the salvation of the souls the missionary wins.

55. Suggest the type of welcome to heaven the Lord will extend to all his servants who have been faithful stewards in life.

BIBLIOGRAPHY

There are available an almost unlimited number of books on stewardship for the convenience of those who would like to go into the subject more fully, but only a few of them can be listed here. The following books will be found worth while, though a number of them are rather old:

Roswell C. Long, *Stewardship Parables of Jesus*
M. E. Melvin, **Royal Partnership*
Guy L. Morrill, **You and Yours*
David McConaughy, **Money, the Acid Test*
Bert Wilson, **The Christian and his Money Problems*
Ralph Cushman, **Dealing Squarely with God*
Ellen Quick Pearce, **Woman and Stewardship*
J. B. Lawrence, **Stewardship Applied to Church Finance*
Robert P. Anderson, **The Way to the Best*
Claire Hill Cooper, *Not Your Own*
Luther E. Lovejoy, **Stewardship for All of Life*
P. E. Burroughs, *Our Lord and Ours*
Julius Earl Crawford, *The Stewardship Life*
F. A. Agar, **The Stewardship of Life*
Charles A. Cook, *Stewardship and Missions*
Charles A. Cook, *The Larger Stewardship*
John D. Freeman, *More Than Money*
William R. Rigell, *Investments in Christian Living*
Walt N. Johnson, **Stewardship Vitalized*
L. R. Scarborough, **A Search for Souls*
P. E. Burroughs, *How to Win to Christ*
R. A. Torrey, *How to Bring Men to Christ*
John D. Freeman and Arthur J. Brown, *Into All the World*
J. L. Corzine, *Fields of Service in the Church*
Egbert W. Smith, **The Desire of All Nations*
M. E. Dodd, **Missions Our Mission*
G. S. Dobbins, *A Winning Witness*

---

*Out of print. See your library.

E. P. Allredge, *The New Challenge of Home Missions
Katherine S. Cronk, *Missionary Methods for Church
  and Home
O. Hallesby, Prayer
Thomas Payne, *The Greatest Force on Earth
M. E. Dodd, *The Prayer Life of Jesus
R. A. Torrey, How to Pray
S. D. Gordon, Quiet Talks on Prayer

YOUNG PEOPLE AND ADULTS

C W. Hatch, Stewardship Enriches Life
Harriet H. Dexter, Financing Faith
B. C. Land, Techniques of a Stewardship Revival
J. B. Lawrence, Stewardship Applied in Missions
Frank K. Means, Give Ye
Paul H. Conrad, Partnership with Christ
John E. Simpson, Stewardship and the World Mission
Helen K. Wallace, Stewardship in the Life of Women
C. Ernest Thomas, To Whom Much Is Given
J. E. Dillard, Bible Stewardship
R. D. Williamson and Helen K. Wallace, Stewardship in
  the Life of Youth
Amy Compere Hickerson, These Dared To Share

CHILDREN

Edith Huckabay, Genny, Penny, and Kan
Josephine R. Medlin, The Steward Family
Martha Jo Walters Milne, Bonny Baptist and the Sun-
  beams

---

*Out of print. See your library.